Ending *Well*

Advice for

successful re-entry

after living abroad

Ellen Rosenberger

Dedication

Dedicated to my Grandmommy, a woman who means the world to me. Her house has always been home to me and she will always be in some of my fondest childhood memories.

Acknowledgments

Alicia Navarrete — for your editing skills and invaluable insight; I'm so grateful for all of your input and for our continued friendship.

Amanda Gutierrez — for your encouragement and help with editing.

Denny Van Deman — for your kindness in aiding with final edits.

Carol Evaul — for cleaning up my manuscript and being like an aunt to me.

Denise Murphy — for being my new friend in my new home; your family is an answer to prayer.

South Fellowship Church and the Summit — for opening your arms and hearts to our family; we are truly blessed to be part of your community.

Luke — for your steadfast love for our family, for encouraging me to pursue my dreams, and for, once again, being the best formatter and cover designer I could hope to work with.

Elizabeth Kate — for slowing me down enough to be reminded of the best things in life.

Table of Contents

Introduction

Reverse culture shock. Loneliness. Expectation. Confusion. Grief. Excitement. Fear. When missionaries or expats return to their home country after any length of time overseas, they often experience these varying emotions. And yet many do not have the tools or the preparation to navigate these tumultuous feelings. Please note that I use the term "missionary" throughout the book because that was my context and my experience. However, the principles apply to a broader range of people: expats, embassy workers, military, global workers of any kind, and even those facing life-altering moves.

Though unique to each individual or family, the transition process carries with it universal struggles. How does one adapt to the passport country after being away? How is home found again? How does a person handle loneliness or misunderstandings from family and friends?

Too often, the complicated and difficult process of re-entry goes overlooked and missionaries are going through it underprepared. Many times it is not a topic of discussion among churches or supporters; therefore, missionaries are going through it with little to no resources and empathy.

In this book I will address the many aspects of re-entry to give hope and resources to missionaries who either are preparing for or are in the middle of re-entry. I will share feasible ideas and steps to take while still in the host country in order to help ensure a smoother landing on the other side. Even if you are on the field and not planning on moving back to your home country in the near future, you most likely will someday. Perhaps you know others who are preparing for a move and would like to offer them practical support.

As a missionary kid who has made countless transitions in my lifetime and then as an adult missionary, I know what it is like to go through the awkwardness, the pain, the newness of re-entry. I've been there. I'm still there. My family moved back to the United States in June of 2016 after serving in Nicaragua for almost twelve years. I know first-hand what the throes of re-entry are like. I write from my own personal experience in addition to the experiences of many friends who made the transition months or years before us.

A healthy, thriving transition is possible. My experience is certainly not a perfect model and none is, but I believe it will serve to show that a healthy transition is possible for you. I pray you will come away from reading this book with encouragement that you can begin your own re-entry with tools that will make for a smooth landing.

I've seen many people wait until they are in the middle of transition to start thinking about how to do it well. Re-entry begins at least six months before you actually board the plane for your passport country. The degree to which you prepare will directly affect how your re-entry unfolds in your home country.

It is my goal as well that mission agencies and churches find this book helpful in better understanding what their missionaries are going through when they return from the field. But not only that, that they will be proactive in helping their missionaries work through the difficulties of re-entry. That they would truly be a support to their missionaries during a time when they most need it.

If you are not a missionary or expat and are reading this book, I applaud you for being intentional in desiring to better understand, relate to, and help a missionary as they are going through the often overwhelming experience of re-entry.

Ending Well is organized into three parts. Part One is all about the leaving, the preparing to move off the mission field. In Part Two I'll address the chaos stage, those initial few weeks and months after returning to the home country. Finally, Part Three focuses on the settling, the getting used to the "new normal." In each part I include journal entries and letters to people as it relates to that specific stage of transition. At the end of each section I have included suggested applications from various chapters.

This is our story. It is not the same as another's. I don't claim to have all the answers or perfect solutions for a smooth sailing transition. I know what has worked for us and I hope you find what works for you. As you enter my story may you be encouraged, empowered and given hope.

ELLEN ROSENBERGER

Part One
The Leaving

"Where we love is home - home that our feet may leave, but not our hearts."

- Oliver Wendell Holmes

ELLEN ROSENBERGER

Chapter 1
Our Story

In order to understand where a person is currently, you have to know a bit about the road they have walked. And so before diving into what our transition back to the States has been like, I want to paint a picture of what our life in Nicaragua was like. I truly believe that your experience of the host country directly affects how you leave it and what memories will remain with you.

My husband, Luke and I met in Nicaragua in the summer of 2005. He had been living there for a year before I got there, teaching at the Christian school where I had come to teach. I arrived in Nicaragua not knowing a single person and I quickly found new friends, including this man who intrigued me so much.

My first few years in Nicaragua were marked by adventure, drama in my relationship with Luke, excitement at trying new things and joy in my place of service. All the while I was rediscovering old rhythms of living in Latin culture being that I had grown up as a missionary kid in Santa Cruz, Bolivia. Luke and I were young, we were single, and we had lots of time to invest in people around us. We were in the honeymoon stage of enjoying our new host country of Nicaragua.

Initially, Luke and I had committed to serving at our Christian school for terms of two and three years. Somehow that commitment ended up extending to twelve. I say somehow, but really I know how it happened. We fell in love with the people, the country, and each other. And we stayed year after year.

We were married in December of 2008 and continued to enjoy ministry alongside each other. Not only were we teaching, but we had become heavily involved in forming and running the youth ministry that was a partnership between our church and school. Those were years of growth and fruit. And time. And no kids of our own.

When our first son, David, was born and we started growing our family, roles started to shift and Luke and I had different experiences of Nicaragua. I was no longer the single teacher serving wholeheartedly and investing heavily in the school. Now I was figuring out what it looked like to be mom, wife, missionary, contributor to our community, etc.

As the years rolled on the fatigue of ministry started to catch up with Luke and myself as well, though I was in more of a support role now. We began seriously considering a furlough which was not a common thing at all at our school. In fact it was pretty uncommon in our missionary community, not talked about much or even encouraged. A lot of people we knew who had "taken a furlough" didn't end up coming back.

But facing burnout and sensing a real direction from God to step out in faith and take a furlough, we did so. We spent the 2014-2015 school year in Indiana recovering from burnout, resting, being a family, spending time with relatives, and thinking a lot about the future and our long-term goals with regard to staying in Nicaragua.

Upon returning to Nicaragua in June of 2015, we felt we were at a crossroads in our future plans. We had decided to return for at least a year and "see after that." It had been our plan to return to Nicaragua all along and we followed through. Going on furlough was not codeword for "we're taking a break to decide whether or not we'll continue living in Nicaragua" as it had seemed for a few others we had known.

Admittedly, I struggled with returning to Nicaragua. My heart was not excited. I remembered well the burnout that we had very recently recovered from. Our financial support had dropped significantly at the same time as our expenses had increased. I was anxious and curious about how much longer we were planning on staying in Nicaragua. Would it be as it had been, just making the decision year by year to continue Luke's contract with the school? What about long-term goals and the shift in roles that I had experienced as we grew a family?

I had a hard time honestly expressing to my husband my resistance to return to Nicaragua. He could sense it though. And in his own way he was uncertain about a number of things upon our return. People, policies, structures and environments had changed in the ministries we had long been involved in. It was painful to grapple with feelings of rejection and discouragement after presenting a vision for ministry and it being denied (or not being approved). Where was my husband's place now? How could he pour his passion into a role that was different than what he had hoped for upon our return?

Due to these feelings we certainly had been tempted to consider staying in the United States but we chose to trust in God. Confident in His sovereignty, goodness, timing and plan for our lives, even though it took all that we were to do so. But regardless of these tensions we made the move back even though it wasn't easy. It was a choice of obedience. My husband is a man of his word, and we said we would return and so return we did.

So, there we were, back in Nicaragua for at least a year, maybe more. But both Luke and I found ourselves at a place of indecision as to how much longer to stay. And how would we know? If I was honest, I had sensed that the roots of my heart that were so strongly grounded in Nicaragua had been gradually pulling up over the past couple of years. The furlough year had been a welcome change for me. Maybe it was because I was used to the pattern of my life as a missionary kid; I was adaptable, always ready for change, for something new. Maybe since my role was less connected to the school now and my primary ministry was my family, I was thinking beyond Nicaragua.

I remember in those first few weeks back in Nicaragua when the transition back was real and fresh, it seemed that Luke and I were constantly talking about our future and the decision to stay or go. Almost obsessively. Not arguing, just talking, re-hashing, dreaming, comparing what we thought.

We finally decided to bring our thoughts and struggles to a trusted older, wiser, more experienced missionary couple. These were dear friends of ours from whom we had learned many things about life and faith. We had also had the privilege of having their kids in our youth group. They listened and gave their input and prayed with us.

What struck me the most about their counsel were two things. First, they told us to take a timeout for about six weeks, agreeing to not talk about it (yes, we could think about it, pray about it on our own, but take a break from constantly discussing it together). This was a boundary that we would establish to give a pause to the problem. Secondly, they encouraged us both to be aware of whether or not our roots were beginning to become re-established here.

I thought that was wise advice. We took them up on it, and it was a good thing we did. The timeout allowed us some space to reflect, providing relief from the urge to constantly be over-analyzing everything, while giving us an opportunity for personal reflection.

When we reopened the discussion about our future plans, Luke and I discovered that neither one of us had a strong sense that our roots were once again being re-established in Nicaragua. In fact it felt very much like the opposite. About a month later, Luke and I had the opportunity of engaging in an all-day event our community termed "R3" (Rest, Reflect, Renew). It was there that we each enjoyed extended time to pray and seek God about our future as well as quality time together to continue working through whether we should go or stay.

During one of the time blocks of the day we decided to each create our own pro's and con's list in order to talk through them together. I wrote out my pro's and con's side by side. I share them here to give you a glimpse of the magnitude of this decision, to leave all we had ever known together, where we had spent our whole adult lives. In many ways, these lists were previews of what we would be grieving should we choose a certain path.

October 3, 2015

Pro's of Staying in Nicaragua:

- We met here
- Our kids were born here
- Comfortable/known
- Kids learn Spanish
- Beautiful house
- Bella (our dog)
- Working vehicle/moto
- Finding more things to do
- Cheap movies
- Potential for feeling settled
- Great doctor care
- TCK (Third Culture Kid) experience for our kids
- Less materialism and a slower paced life
- Great school to work at

- Lots of history and memories here
- Great community/church to be part of

Con's of Staying in Nicaragua:

- Don't necessarily want to
- Always wondering when our time is up
- Fundraising/role of missionary
- Many close friends have left
- Not excited about being here anymore
- Hot, frustrated, tired, critical
- Feels "against my will"
- Struggling with feeling unneeded/unwanted
- School and church community changing
- Feeling stuck and left behind
- "Old hat"
- Feeling undervalued
- Eventually more friends will probably leave
- Far away from family
- Very little activities and resources for kids
- Aren't we just prolonging leaving?

Pro's of Leaving Nicaragua:

- Excitement
- Fresh start (together)
- No fundraising, communication responsibilities (I can focus on my family)
- Closer to family
- Better/more resources for kids
- Feel ready for this change
- Do not dread it, want it!

- Better fit for Luke?
- Better situation for our family?
- We get to learn together, expand our experience
- See God provide
- "Grow up"
- New adventure
- More restful place (?) (as far as not any cultural burnout to deal with)
- Beginning a new chapter (that feels has already started)

Con's of Leaving Nicaragua:

- Saying goodbye to people and memories (though in some ways they already seem gone, like another lifetime)
- Fear of regret, making a mistake in leaving
- Leaving our comfort zone
- The unknown
- Kids miss out on TCK experience and Spanish
- Will take a few years to get our feet on the ground, figure out a new life

This exercise of listing out pro's and con's provided a place for me to be painfully honest with myself as well as with Luke, an area where I had been growing during recent years. I had experienced the damaging effects of using my own coping mechanisms by concealing my true thoughts. I discovered that I had done this because I was afraid of what others might think. I had a tendency to be a people pleaser because I did not want to complicate relationships. But I had been gradually experiencing the freedom in being honest, especially in situations where I had to express my real concerns in order to find solutions.

Putting the pro's and con's down on paper opened up a new way for me to wrestle with all of my thoughts, emotions, and true feelings about the different aspects of the decision. It helped us move forward on the practical level of making our decision, which as seen from many of the conflicted statements in this list, was not easy.

As we wrestled with the decision to stay or go, we battled the real emotions of guilt and fear. Guilt over even considering leaving. Fear of what others would say. *What would others think? How would they respond? Did it look like we were giving up? If we were to choose to leave, would our news be received with an attitude of "man, someone else is leaving us"?*

Luke is a faithful and committed person. For him, considering leaving felt like he was being a traitor. In a community where people come and go frequently, he had been among the few who had chosen to stay. He was a pillar of faithful service, fiercely committed to his youth group kids, and deeply invested in their lives and the mission of the school and church. When seemingly all around him was changing and people were leaving, he had remained. I know from the experience of growing up as a missionary kid that having a role model who is constant in the midst of change is invaluable.

Being part of such a transient community for so long has its effects on how you view people staying and leaving. There's almost this underlying holding of breath around certain times of the year, like when the school year is coming to an end. *Who will it be next? When's the next announcement going to come out?* And we hold tightly to those we know who are staying because they are reliable, they are predictable, at least they are not leaving (yet). Now it was us who were considering the leaving. We were the ones who would be disappointing others.

The guilt was heavy and the fear of others' responses was real. And, honestly, these were emotions we had to continue to battle even after we made our decision. But we did not let them be reasons to stay. We pressed through them into what we believed God was leading us to, though it was hard.

And so through all of the prayers, the counsel, the thinking, the pro's and con's lists, God was gracious to bring us to a place *together* where we each felt peace about our time in Nicaragua coming to a close. But thankfully, not only did we both sense that it was right for us to move on from Nicaragua at that time, but there was a path ahead being illuminated.

Luke's spirit was stirred up again toward seminary studies (something he had been considering in recent years), and he felt strongly drawn to Denver Seminary in Littleton, Colorado. Though he had many years of youth pastoring experience, a desire had kept resurfacing, a desire to study the Bible, to become more trained and to learn and grow and be mentored himself. The idea of studying the Bible full time and being poured into and learning was really appealing to him. He felt an excitement in his spirit and heart that he had not experienced in recent years. Luke realized that regardless of his location in this world, he wanted to be involved in God's kingdom work, in pastoral ministry whether that be with youth, families, or in a missions capacity.

We felt a peace about Luke applying to seminary, and we trusted God with the details. He was accepted, and we began making plans to move our family to Colorado. Though we didn't know many people in Colorado aside from Luke's sister and her family, we felt a similar draw to it as we each had to Nicaragua when deciding to move there all those years ago. An intrigue, an excitement, a sense of "this is right, this is good."

I believe our decision would have felt differently if we had not had a clear picture of what we were stepping into for the future. Having something to be excited about and plan for helped immensely in the leaving process. It would have been completely different if we were leaving because of burn-out or with feelings of failure and defeat.

Though it took awhile to arrive at the decision to move to the States, when we officially did make it we were blessed with a sense of relief, peace, joy and excitement. But those were accompanied with feelings of sadness, finality, grief. This was the close of a significant chapter in our lives, and it was okay to recognize the paradox of feeling excitement at the same time as feeling sadness. Colorado here we come! But Nicaragua we're already missing you.

There are countless reasons why missionaries leave the field, and the circumstances surrounding their departure. I fully believe that those circumstances are key components as to how they will re-enter their home country. Was the decision made in an emergency? What were the reasons for leaving (both stated reasons and those left unsaid)? All are major factors.

If you are an expat, I don't know what your experience has been in your host country. Maybe it was mostly positive, or maybe it was characterized by substantial loss and difficulty. I don't know how long you were there, what your relationship was like with your colleagues and the people you served, or even how you went through the process of deciding to leave. For some that decision was made for them. Either by a spouse or a mission agency because of interpersonal conflict, a political situation, health issues or a natural disaster.

Luke and I were different people when we arrived in Nicaragua and when we left. We experienced many highs and lows, joys and trials, adventures, and goodbyes during our time there. All of this influenced how our transition off the field went. And our transition began the moment we made the decision to leave. For us that was about six months before we moved.

So here we go. The decision has been made, but we haven't left yet. What is involved in "the leaving," the preparing for this major life move? What helped us to leave well? In the next few chapters I'll talk about the specific ways we said goodbye to people and places in Nicaragua and how that played an important role in helping us leave well. Why is leaving well important? Because I've experienced that it is directly connected to arriving well. If you want to arrive well, be intentional about leaving well.

ELLEN ROSENBERGER

Chapter 2
Saying Goodbye to People

"Bye bye, I love you."

Not too long ago, Luke and I realized we routinely say this to each other or to our kids whenever we are leaving to go somewhere. Whether it is for a short or long time. It had become almost an automatic phrase, like a knee-jerk reaction to a departure. Not that it was devoid of meaning and emotion; it was just what we always said when we left the other.

I started to think about how interesting it is that sometimes it takes a departure for us to express our love and affection to another. Preparing to leave your host country is an opportune time to intentionally express love to those who have meant the most to you, those who have been your family when family was miles away. May we regularly express our gratitude to those we love in the middle of normal life, not only before a big goodbye.

Before I get into specific ways Luke and I were intentional with saying goodbye to people and how that helped our transition be a healthy one, I want to highlight some of the initial reactions people can have when they find out you are leaving. You cannot control others' reactions and that's okay. You'll be better off mentally and emotionally if you do not try to and just allow their reactions to be what they are.

You can expect that there will be different responses depending on the person and on your level of friendship. Each person expresses grief differently. Some people will, in order to protect themselves from hurt, pull back from a relationship. Others will express shock and even anger.

We were thankful that, as far as we could tell, our closest friends were excited for us and the ways God was leading our family. Yes, they expressed sadness over saying goodbye to doing everyday life together, but they were looking forward to hearing how God was going to provide on the other side.

The regular reaction we got from Nicaraguans was "You don't like it here?" Instead of being offended by these comments, we chose to expect this response and see it as their own processing of the news mixed in with some hurt pride.

Still others might react quite insensitively and immediately begin inquiring about the stuff you will have for sale before you leave. No joke, a friend of mine told me that after an acquaintance had found out that her family would be moving back to the States, in the same breath of saying something like "You'll be missed," immediately asked if she could buy my friend's dryer. I understand that appliances are expensive, and dryers are a rare commodity in Nicaragua (and especially helpful during the rainy season where hanging clothes out on the line is not necessarily impossible but definitely a dance of extreme calculation and planning) but really? At least wait a day. Don't ask about it in the same conversation. But as this woman knew from experience, you have to act fast or you'll miss out on a good deal. In situations like this, it's so important to extend grace. This can save you from annoyance and frustration.

Be wise in how and when you tell others. We made sure that we told those closest to us in person. We did not want them to find out on their own through the missionary grapevine. We even let a few in on the possibility of our move while we were still praying through the decision. Telling personally those who are closest to you honors them and will help eliminate chances of their reacting in shock and anger. You can avoid a lot of miscommunication about the real reasons why you are leaving if you directly and personally tell others.

So, how were we intentional about saying goodbye to people? First off, the steps we took were not original to us. In our years overseas we had seen plenty of people come and go. We'd seen goodbyes done well, and we'd seen goodbyes done poorly. I don't think we were quite thinking about it at the time, but perhaps mentally we were storing up tips on how to leave well as modeled by others.

One of the first things Luke and I did was make a list of the most important people in our lives, those people who had become like family to us, the ones who deserved the highest priority of time before we left. This might sound "choosy" or steeped in exclusivity but believe me, it is important. Why? Because if you don't have a prioritized list, you will spend the last few weeks or days running around trying to please everyone whoever says to you, "We should get together sometime before you leave." Which they will. Even if you hardly ever spent time together in country, they will suddenly want to hang out during the busiest of days as you are scrambling to get your house moved out of, travel documents together, bags and heart packed up for flight. A group gathering, such as an official goodbye party, is a great event to invite these people to. They get to see you one last time, and you don't need to feel guilty about not spending individual time with them.

It's okay to prioritize the important people in your life. It will honor them, and it will save you stress and guilt in the last days. So we took this list of most important people and looked at our calendar. We knew the last few weeks and days would be filled with last minute errands: bank accounts to close, residency cards to relinquish, and countless other things we couldn't do until the very end.

So we got time with these special people on the calendar early. We made sure it would be quality time we could enjoy together, doing activities we were accustomed to enjoy together (whether it was playing games, watching a movie or being outdoors). Often we would combine the time together with saying goodbye to a particular place such as the beach or my favorite spot of all, a calm and clear crater lake called Laguna de Apoyo only an hour from the city.

Another way that I personally chose to be intentional about saying goodbye to people was through letter writing. I wrote to those who had influenced me, blessed me or been a significant friend over the years. I wanted to thank, appreciate, and honor them. I'm not gifted with spoken words, but I find expression through writing. I knew I could give the gift of encouragement and honor friendships through letter writing. I wrote about the memories we'd shared, what I appreciated about each one of them and what I would uniquely miss about them.

As I wrote, I discovered that the exercise was as much for me as it was for them. It helped put my grief into words, to process what I would be losing when I said goodbye, and it gave me a tangible way to praise God for the blessing of their friendship. I remember being on the receiving end of a few goodbye letters from friends who had left before me. To me it was an incredible gift that the person would take the time out of their busy schedule of packing and getting ready for their move to put onto paper what I meant to them. I prayed my letters did the same.

I even decided to write a letter to our dog, Bella, who was like our first kid and who we sadly had to leave in Nicaragua. I also wrote a letter to the country of Nicaragua as a way to process my leaving of my home of so many years. You can find these at the end of this section in chapter six.

At the same time as I was writing letters and saying goodbye to people who were still in Nicaragua, in my mind I was rehashing goodbyes to the many close friends I had let go of through the years. We had said our goodbyes long ago, and they had moved on and started a new chapter in a new home. But I had been left here, in this place with these memories. In an odd way these relationships had lived on in a sense through these physical places, these reminders of special times with friends.

Now I found myself reliving their departures and thinking of each of them every time I passed that one bench where we had shared conversations after school, that hiking trail we had frequented, that classroom we had spent time in, that house filled with memories of pizza and movies on the weekends.

Soon I wouldn't be surrounded by the constant reminder of these significant people in my life. I would have to say the final goodbye. When you've lived in a place for so long, and it comes time for your departure, sometimes it feels that there's no one left to say goodbye to you. You've been on this side of goodbyes for so long and now that it's your turn, who is there to see you off?

Another intentional step Luke and I took in saying goodbye to people was making sure we were on good terms with them. We spent the time and emotional energy it required to make it right with whom we had had any kind of conflict. We fought hard against the temptation to allow bitterness and anger characterize our leaving. We chose to work through conflict and tension, meeting with the elders at our church to move toward reconciliation and understanding rather than running in the opposite direction and saying "we're leaving, it doesn't matter anyway."

It would have been easier not to deal with the hurt and the messiness of human relationships but we wanted for our sakes and theirs not to have any regrets when leaving. We did not want to leave bitter or angry. We wanted to leave on good terms, and we knew this would be good for our relationships and for our own emotional well being.

It's been said that missionary conflict is one of the top reasons people leave the mission field, and it's not hard to see why. If you're currently in a situation of conflict or have been in the past, I urge you not to wait. Dealing with the problems, the people, the situation before you leave is so much healthier than leaving without peaceful closure. This is the time to offer forgiveness, to ask questions, to seek understanding and unity, to apologize. Unresolved issues will likely haunt you after you've moved half a world away, and they are much more difficult to work through when you are not face to face.

We were intentional about saying goodbye to people by being careful not to say goodbye too early. It's tempting to want to check out early. After all, in the months leading up to your departure, your mind is easily consumed with plans for your future world as you are making decisions on housing, schooling, and jobs. It can be natural and even a coping mechanism to be physically present in your host country while your mind and heart are already in your new place.

Luke and I did not want this to happen to us. We wanted to stay present. To stay invested in where we were currently living even as we were simultaneously making plans and securing details for our new home. We resisted the urge to check out, and instead, we did not forgo activities and opportunities to be involved in our community and in ministry.

On the contrary, we not only engaged in what was going on around us, but we initiated many new community and service activities. I enjoyed hosting a fall sale in my home where expat women could gather for a morning of craft shopping, fellowship and food. We loved opening up our home for an Easter sunrise service filled with prayer and singing. Luke continued to lead retreats, teach Sunday school, and he preached a few times at our church. We organized a group of elementary kids to help lead worship a few

Sundays. I enjoyed introducing and leading a unique idea of Christmas gift-giving at a ministry for children with disabilities.

We became friends with people who were new to Nicaragua, a rare action in a community where goodbyes are frequent, and it's common to shield your heart from further pain by resisting new relationships. Looking back, we're grateful we invested in new friendships, and we can see the joy and fellowship we would have forfeited had we decided to not take that risk.

Our family stayed connected. And we did so out of joy, not obligation or guilt. This is part of what made our last year in Nicaragua a healthy and strong one, almost like a "victory lap." A year we enjoyed and took opportunities to be grateful, to reminisce, to engage.

It would certainly have been easier to disengage, to protect ourselves from the impending pain of goodbyes. Why create more memories if we knew we were only going to leave them in a few months? Because it was worth it. Yes, it was hard to say goodbye, but it was sweet to say goodbye, knowing we had not held back. We didn't want the alternative: saying goodbye prematurely and being left with seeds of resentment and regret. We didn't want to dishonor or embitter those around us by living with an attitude of "hurry up, let's get out of here."

We were careful to be sensitive to those around us by not speaking too often of our upcoming move. Instead, we made sure to be interested in their lives, what was going on with them, the plans and dreams they had. We'd been on the other side of things before where we were the ones being left. It's not so fun to hear constantly of the new adventure awaiting someone who will be leaving you soon. You can honor others by remaining sensitive to them and what life stage they are in currently.

And so we stayed present in our current life and community. And I cannot tell you how much that influenced how our transition continued to go. Living with not one regret, enjoying our host culture and the people we loved until the last day, not leaving early. All of those intentional ways of saying goodbye well were like healthy deposits on the other end of our transition.

I know it's not easy and it takes work and intentionality, but stay present. Verbally affirm those who have meant the most to you. Take care of conflict now. Don't leave too early. Live out your last days in your host country with no regrets. Your future self in your future transition will thank you for it.

Chapter 3
Saying Goodbye to Places and Things

Much like we did with the significant people in our life, Luke and I made a list of places to visit one last time. Though places are not people, they still harbor important memories from the span of years lived abroad. We thought of every possible place that held significance to us (even if we hadn't been there in years), and we put it on that list.

The site of our first date (which is ironically a sushi restaurant, and neither of us love sushi). The pupusa restaurant out of someone's home that the kids loved to go to after preschool to get $1 pupusas (a delicious food native to El Salvador). The beach where our dog loved to run free and our kids collected hermit crabs. The mall where everyone we knew would hang out on the weekends because there aren't that many options for entertainment in Managua. The market with its crowds and smells and glorious bustle. The theater with its tall white pillars, a symbol of history and class sitting opposite the port, a contrast of old and new life in Managua. Our favorite running route in our neighborhood, winding through hard, dirt streets and filled with sounds of life: people, babies, dogs, chickens, soccer and baseball games.

Luke compiled the list on his phone so we could add to it as we were out and about whenever an idea would pop into our minds. We could see each location crossed off as we hit them. It didn't matter if the place was a restaurant, a store, or would take a whole day to visit, we put it on the list. And we began going to these places over the course of several months before we left. We had to intentionally find time on the calendar to do these things because otherwise it wasn't going to happen. We didn't wait to cram it all in the last two weeks.

As we visited each place we took pictures and enjoyed our last moments there. We reminisced about the special times we'd shared in each place and who we'd shared them with. A friend of ours who has moved back to the States from Nicaragua shared with me once that when he revisited favorite places he chose to pretend like a tourist and really take in the view. This gave him a new appreciation for the scenery and gave him fond memories to take with him.

We involved our kids in our goodbyes to places as well. During our final days in Nicaragua our son David would often say, "Is this our last time at this place or that place?" He knew we'd been saying goodbye to places for months, and he wanted to know when it would be the last visit to each place.

Sometimes we combined a place with saying goodbye to special people if we had memories connected there. For example, Luke said goodbye to one of his best friends at a quesillo restaurant as they savored the cheesy Nicaraguan favorite like they had done so many times before.

A few times we combined places we had been to many times before with friends who had never been there. It was fun to create new memories with our friends; we were saying goodbye, but they were experiencing a place for the first time. For example, we enjoyed returning to an old favorite, Cañon de Somoto, a beautiful, secluded place we had discovered early on in our single years. Now years later we returned to say goodbye along with our kids and good friends who had never been there before.

As we said goodbye to all of these places we involved our family and sometimes other friends, but there was one place that Luke and I went to alone. It was a place that had been a hope of mine to visit for many years: Corn Island. Having lived in Nicaragua for years I had always heard of Corn Island and wanted to go sometime.

But life and kids and finances and schedules all happened, and I had never gone. Luke had been twice before; one of those times he was helping lead a mission trip. Well, we decided it was time. When else would we go? We were in country now. Soon we would be much farther away from Corn Island. Who knows when we'd ever get another chance?

So, we left our kids and went on a four-day adventure on the other side of Nicaragua, which really felt like another country. A hello to a different side of Nicaragua and a goodbye to the country as a whole. A chance to reminisce and enjoy with this husband of mine whom I had met here so many years earlier.

We went about two weeks before moving to the States, so it gave us a good goal of getting a lot of things done on our "to-do" lists before the trip to Corn Island in order to be able to fully enjoy it. It was a little after I had published my first book so this trip was a celebration.

The weekend we traveled to Corn Island happened to be exactly nine years to the day of when Luke and I started officially dating (made official by a phone call while he was actually on his way to Corn Island). He said in that phone call "I want to take you to Corn Island someday." And now nine years later there we were experiencing that part of the country together on the brink of moving our family to another world.

Taking time away was beneficial for our emotional well-being and ultimately was a big part of helping our transition during the chaos stage go smoother. There are no words to describe the value in those four days of calm, of reflection, of exploration and of enjoyment. They were especially key because of the chaos of transition that was about to hit in the coming weeks. Like a calm before the storm. We had time to enjoy this beautiful country on our own without kids and time to reflect back on the past while looking ahead to the future.

Of course there were expenses involved for that big trip and all these other visits to favorite restaurants, stores, and special spots around Managua and the country. We almost didn't go to Corn Island. We almost let fear and guilt and worry over finances make our decision for us (but thankfully we were able to save months in advance and had a number of financial provisions come through prior to the trip). But the expense was well worth it. It was worth it to say goodbye. To remember. To recognize that each place held special memories of time periods and people and milestones in our lives. And soon we would be on a plane flying far, far away from it all. We wanted to enjoy them and say goodbye now, not face regret later.

But those are all external places. Places we'd visited or frequented often. What about the place of the home? The place where we lived, interacted, and spent most of our time? Our home was by far one of the hardest places to say goodbye to. Granted, we had only lived there for a year, since returning from furlough.

Oh, but this home. The breathtaking beauty. Situated on a hill overlooking a beautiful valley, filled with all kinds of trees, bushes, flowers, and the occasional herd of cows or goats. This house, facing the east so that the morning's sunrise could be enjoyed along with the calls of birds and the fresh smell of earth. This house, designed by a Frenchman married to a Nicaraguan, that had splashes of flavor from both Europe and Central America: high wooden ceilings, a courtyard with a pond, oddly placed rooms, banisters and a loft. This house, with ivy growing on the outside walls and the surrounding yard calling daily to our children. This house, the privacy, the natural beauty, the quietness. You could almost forget that you lived on the fringes of busy and hot Managua. As my good friend and former renter of the house perfectly described it once: "this house sings God's peace."

Every single day after making the decision to move, Luke and I literally said to each other "But this house!" I found myself half-jokingly telling people "We would stay for the house alone!" But we knew we couldn't. God had made clear the path before us and was exciting us about the open doors of seminary and possible internships at a church in Littleton, Colorado. And so say goodbye to our beloved Casita, we must.

We chose to enjoy our little house each and every day before leaving. That was our goodbye: living in it, enjoying making memories with the kids and our dog, breathing the smells and being amazed at each sunrise. We knew we might never live in such a place of beauty and versatility for our kids again, but we chose to rejoice in the one year we were blessed to be able to live there with our family.

What about things? Our earthly possessions? How did we say goodbye to and part with those? Everyone's situation differs with how much they are able to take with them. Between our own allotment of suitcases and others we could send back with a missions team, we were able to transport our family of five's life's possessions in eleven suitcases. This, of course, is no smfall feat and required us to really prioritize what was important to us. What things would we keep, sell, give away, throw away? How would we decide?

What helped us immensely was starting early. Getting organized months ahead of time and having a plan. We flew at the end of June, but we made our list of furniture items for sale in January and had all of the items spoken for by March. One thing that we had seen another missionary family do is offer their items for sale to their closest friends and missionaries within their own organization first and then to the rest of the expat community. We decided to do the same as a way of honoring those who were closest to us. One good friend commented that she had always been disappointed when finding out about things for sale too late and they were mostly all claimed. It meant a lot to her that she had first pick on our stuff. We offered our list to the Nicaraguan community before the greater expat community and were amazed at their gratefulness for having the opportunity at buying cheap appliances when they normally miss out on deals like these.

As we priced our household items and furniture, we decided to offer them at lower prices than was the norm. We'd experienced over the years that missionaries usually would price their items close to what they paid for them and understandably so. Moving internationally is costly. The missionary salary is not a large one, and each dollar helps to put towards replacing each item. There is a high demand for good-working appliances and nice furniture and since there aren't many places like Goodwill or the Salvation Army, missionary garage sales are it. But they can still be considerably pricey.

Luke and I wanted to be different. We believed that yes, we could ask for a higher price on many of our things but that we didn't need to. We decided to ask a lower price as a way to bless others. Was this easy? No, it was a step of faith and a declaration of trust that God would provide all we needed for our new home. But we had seen Him provide in amazing ways during our furlough year.

We had gone to the States for that year of rest with only clothes to wear and in need of a furnished house. Can you believe that the only two big items we purchased for that year were a microwave and a kitchen table? Everything else, I mean *everything else* was given. Either by a friend of a family member or a church member or a complete stranger. Beds, cribs, dressers, a vacuum cleaner, a couch. You name it. Even a van to drive and a place to live. We had experienced this incredible provision, and we were trusting that God would provide in similar ways when we got to the other side. Either through donations or even cheap prices at garage sales or Goodwill.

We discovered joy at selling our things for cheap to people we knew would use them. It was freeing not to be in the quest to get the most money out of every big and small item. We took joy in giving away certain special items out of our home to people we wanted to bless. We wanted them to have a physical memory of us, something they would look at in their homes and remember us by. We involved our kids in this process as well as they exercised giving and sacrifice by choosing prized toys to share with friends.

Our oldest is especially tied to his possessions so this was a difficult task. However, with encouragement and practice, he really made us proud by how he ended up taking the initiative to gift toys to friends all the while saying things such as "That was hard for me, Mom, but I know that my friend will love this toy" or "It's okay that I said goodbye to that toy, Dad, because I know it will make this friend happy."

In those eleven suitcases we couldn't pack much, but we kept what was most important: memories. We could easily replace certain clothes, shoes, toys, and books. But that picture, that favorite stuffed animal, that photo album, my favorite little white wall shelf, the hand-made Nicaraguan key holder, even the kids' shower curtain (because it was light and cute and would be something familiar for them in a new place) made the cut. Everything else was said goodbye to, and we recognized with gratitude that we had enjoyed the use of them and now it was time for someone else to benefit from them.

Being intentional and organized about saying goodbye to places and things really helped our moving preparations to run smoothly. We even had one day scheduled out where people who had bought our furniture were to come by to pick it up. That way it was not chaotic with communication and having to arrange to be places at certain times; it all happened on the same day. For your sake and others' you do not want to be running around taking care of payments and pickups and trying to sell last-minute items.

There's something to be said about not leaving undone business or unsold items for others in your organization to deal with after you've gone. Of course in emergency situations this is understandably different, but part of leaving well is taking care of all your business ahead of time so that others aren't left with unfinished tasks and a bad taste in their mouths. It's a way of honoring them and saying goodbye well so that your memory is not attached to the things you left behind for them to do or the lose ends they had to take care of.

The importance of being intentional about saying goodbye to people and places cannot be understated. Doing this well can help ensure you will carry fond memories with you to your new home. In the next chapter I will look at how to prepare yourself emotionally for a move back to your passport country. There are many different layers involved in a move of this kind, and it is extremely important to be proactive in recognizing and expressing how you are doing with all of the impending changes coming your way.

Chapter 4
Preparing Emotionally

In any kind of move, and especially an international one, there are countless tasks to be accomplished. Bags to pack, possessions to sell, tickets to buy, plans to make. But there's something of equal value if not more important: taking care of the heart and mind. Proverbs 4:23 says, "Keep your heart with all vigilance, for from it flow the springs of life." Even if you have only lived abroad for a year, you cannot ignore how your experience has affected you emotionally.

Preparing yourself emotionally is key to preparing yourself for the move. It's not always easy; it takes intentionality and honesty, but it is well worth it. In the end it will do wonders in preparing a smoother landing for you on the other side. First, I'll talk about ways to prepare yourself emotionally on an individual level and secondly how to involve other significant people in your life.

One of the ways that I prepared was through journaling. Oftentimes my journaling is in prayer form as I express my emotions to God, who hears all and sees all, who knows the state of my heart and all that I am experiencing. When I journal I'm actively dealing with the issues I am facing and am aware of the emotions I am experiencing.

The following journal entry was written at a retreat about a month and a half before we left Nicaragua. We were taught about Psalm 42 which is a psalm of lament that moves through three stages:

1. Praising God (language of gratitude)
2. Complaint (what's not matching up)
3. Trusting in God (affirmation of truth)

We were then directed to compose our own psalm of lament for our own life situation.

My Psalm of Lament

Lord, You are good and your mercy endures forever. Lord, You are near to all who call on You, to all who call on You in truth. Jesus, You know me through and through. You know my longings, desires, griefs, joys, insecurities and hopes.

Why must I feel so lonely? Why do I have to go through grief and goodbyes? Why do I feel alone and overlooked...like no one will miss me when I'm gone? Why do I have to be sad about leaving Nicaragua? Why do I feel unwanted, unneeded? Why do I feel gone already? Why do I feel like I'm going to run out of time and not get to do all I want to do and spend time with those I want to remember well?

And yet I will trust You. I will trust You with my grief, with my tears, with my loneliness, with my future. I will trust You for provision of new friends. I will trust You with my sadness and my fear that I won't find things and people in the new land to fill that gap of sadness and loneliness. I trust You with my fear that my loneliness will not go away and might increase in the new land. You are God. You are in charge and You know what I need. You delight in providing for my needs. I will trust that You will provide finances, friendships and peace for our family.

I found a great outlet in writing my first book, *Missionaries Are Real People*, which was written and published during the few months before we moved away from Nicaragua. My book-writing experience was a wonderful way for me to intentionally reflect on my time overseas, think on the lessons learned and pass them on to others in hopes of encouraging and empowering them in their own journeys.

For me, writing has a unique way of sifting through my thoughts and giving me an outlet for expression, for exploration, for making sense of life. As I'm writing, I'm reflecting, I'm learning, I'm understanding. And it helps me look back on experiences with clarity.

Maybe you're not going to write a book, but you like to blog or jot down thoughts from time to time. Any way that you can express what's going on internally will keep you aware of how your heart is doing during this important state of preparing to leave the field.

Another way to prepare emotionally is through reading helpful resources. Luke and I read the book *Re-entry* by Peter Jordan as we embarked on our furlough year. Even though we knew we were only going to be in the States for eleven months, we wanted to be prepared for the re-entry process and all the facets of transition that were coming our way. It's a short, easy read with some practical tips.

A good friend of ours (who made the transition back to the United States six months before us) sent us a copy of *Returning Well* by Melissa Chaplin. This comprehensive and practical resource is in workbook form and is so helpful for thinking through the process of transitions.

Another helpful book is *Looming Transitions* by Amy Young. She speaks honestly and practically about how to prepare yourself for the mess of transition.

Who Moved My Cheese? by Spencer Johnson is a short, easy read and while not specific to missionary life at all, it is a creative story about how different people react to change in their lives. My dad gave me this book when I was beginning college, and it is applicable across the board for anyone, anywhere who is facing a life change whether that be vocationally or relationally or geographically.

Other great resources can be speakers, podcasts, and retreats. Another experience that helped me prepare emotionally was sitting under the wisdom of a women's retreat speaker who taught about the children of Israel moving from Egypt into the wilderness before they took possession of the Promised Land. I found many correlations and applications to my own life as we were about to embark on our own journey into a new land.

The retreat speaker talked about how our story is not just events over time, but an encounter with a place. She called them our "story places." One exercise we did was to draw or diagram what each of our "story places" looked like. I could identify with this concept as I had grown up and lived in a variety of different places. She described missionaries as sojourners in this world and that the main characteristic of a sojourner was that they were never belonging.

She talked about the concept of the wilderness, how it was an unwelcome surprise since the Israelites were not promised this. They were heading to the Promised Land but got stuck in the wilderness. I reflected on our own journey and realized that maybe our transition time in the States could feel like a wilderness. The retreat speaker went on to elaborate that the wilderness is the place where intimacy is created, where having nothing you are lacking nothing. She taught that the Promised Land is not the ultimate gift, but that the ultimate gift is the presence of the Lord. Because God was with the Israelites in the wilderness, they were protected and their needs are provided for.

As I listened I was given courage to go through the wilderness because I knew it was a gift, a profound, painful, important place. That I would not be abandoned in the wilderness. That I could cross over into the land like they did and let go. She talked about how God does not promise absence of threats but He promises presence, provision and protection. The speaker talked about our actions and attitude in the new land. She said that gratitude is the language of the Promised Land, of rootedness; it's the second language we need to learn. And then she encouraged us to practice hospitality in the new land. I loved this quote by her: "Hospitality doesn't wait to be settled to extend kindness."

As a result of the retreat, I resolved to enter into my new land with gratitude and to recognize God's presence even if it felt like we were alone. I felt strongly that I should strive to offer hospitality to others and not simply wait on others to reach out to me. This was counter-intuitive in my mind. *Shouldn't I be the one being welcomed in? I don't know these people. I'm going to be so out of my element.* But I felt a joyful motivation to take the first step toward extending hospitality, whether it be through inviting others into our home, making a meal, or initiating a hello. Hospitality didn't have to be restricted to our physical home; it could be the mindset of inviting others into our lives and hearts.

Another key component to personally preparing for returning to your home country is recognizing grief and loss. Know that grief doesn't only happen when a loved one passes away. Grief happens at the loss of any number of things: a job, a home, friends, purpose, a life you've known for many years. And it's okay to enter into that grief. In fact, it's much better for your heart to specifically identify what you are losing and allow yourself to grieve. One of the best pieces of advice I heard just after I had moved away from Bolivia to begin college life in the United States was: "Give yourself permission to grieve."

Please don't ignore grief. Know that the grieving begins even before your plane takes off from your host country. It may even intensify in your new place. Choose to enter into the place of grief, to cry out to God in your grief and thank Him for the blessing of those people you miss, that home you left behind, the life that is over for now. I read a book called *Parenting Is Heart Work* by Dr. Scott Turansky and Joanne Miller, and in it I found a wonderful statement about the purpose of grief. They say, "grief is the emotional tool God gives us to release the things we value." I found that to be a freeing, life-giving, and honoring description of an emotion that can be uncomfortable and unwanted. If I could look at it as a gift, a tool, a way to honor the people and things that I love, I could enter into it with a much different attitude and mindset.

Probably one of the biggest losses that a missionary experiences when moving off the field is a loss of identity. In my first book I wrote an entire chapter on how our identity as missionaries is wrapped up in what we do, our work, our ministry. Who we are and what we do become inseparable. *Do we know how to live without the title "missionary"? Who are we now?*

Take time to recognize where your self-worth lies, where your purpose is. Is it solely in what you do, how you serve, who you are as a missionary? Or are you grounded and rooted in something deeper than that? Because if you're not standing on who God says you are (apart from your missionary role), re-entry is going to be doubly hard as you try to figure out who you are now that your identity has been seemingly stripped away.

Even if you are in a healthy place of recognizing your worth in Christ apart from what you do, be aware that there will still be struggles in this area. Grappling with your identity is a natural part of grieving who you once were as opposed to the place you are in now.

I share the following journal entry as an insight into how, a few months after I moved to Colorado, I processed this loss of identity.

October 28, 2016

Yesterday I felt like curling up in a ball and going back to where I came from. Where it's familiar. Where I'm known, understood, and appreciated. In Nicaragua I was competent. I knew what I was doing. There were roles to fill and few people to do them. I rarely felt unfit or incompetent. I felt fulfilled, confident, comfortable. Not so now. I'm battling thoughts of insecurity and embarrassment. I feel strange and out of place. I feel exposed and like I should know more and have more refined skills. I miss Nicaragua. I miss being accepted and at peace there. I miss being comfortable and not challenged too much there. I miss knowing who I was and what I could do there. It's hard to figure these things out....this thing of who I am here. And yet my heart is reminded that I am the same here as I was there. I am loved. I am God's child. I am delighted in. I've been given skills and talents. I am redeemed by the blood of the Lamb. I am a citizen of Heaven along with all my other brothers and sisters who have different talents than me. I belong to Jesus.

Recognize that the feelings of loss of identity will be a struggle and a tension. Use the opportunity now to build truth into your mindset of who you are. Though your circumstances, responsibilities, and purpose will be changing soon, remind yourself that you are still a child of God, created in His image, loved and cared for immensely by Him. Your worth in His eyes has nothing to do with what you do or where you live.

In whatever way you choose to individually process and express your emotions in preparation for your move, choose to be honest. Even if it's hard. It's tempting to avoid the impending pain of goodbyes and the inevitability of change but it is much healthier to actively and honestly deal with what is coming and what is already happening in your heart.

Not only is it important to have self-awareness as you move toward re-entry, but it is incredibly helpful and healthy to involve others on your journey. So don't keep what you are processing to yourself. Talk with others. Involve your friends, family, and supporters. Share with them what you are processing and ask them to pray for specific areas of your life as you prepare for your move.

If you are married, be open with your spouse. He or she is the one who will be traveling this journey closest to you and can be an incredible source of encouragement and mutual understanding as you navigate through this season. If you are single, be intentional to seek out a good friend or confidant who can journey with you through the emotions of re-entry. Be bold to ask for what you need in their friendship during this pivotal time.

Ask questions of others who have gone through the re-entry process ahead of you. We found incredible value in listening to other friends' re-entry experiences. We gained many insights into what we might expect or pitfalls we could avoid. Stay in touch with these friends who have gone before you as they can be valuable resources and encouragement.

I think the most important thing you can do is plan for a debriefing time. Get this on the calendar before you land in your home country. Knowing that you will have this intentional time will help immensely as you emotionally prepare for the move. Sometimes these programs are focused more on individual counseling and reflection, but many times they involve being part of a group of others with whom you can process your transition. Others who get it, who are right there with you.

I cannot recommend a debriefing time highly enough! On the onset of our furlough year Luke and I decided to attend Debriefing and Renewal (DAR) at Mission Training International. And we are so glad that we did. The tools for working through grief and transition we learned that week, the empathy we received from others, the counsel we were given and the space and time to process our re-entry were an absolute gift.

It was there that we learned about the stages of transition, what to look for and what to expect. It was there that we found others who had similar stories and struggles as us though they had lived on the other side of the world. It was there that we gained hope and perspective that we could survive and even thrive during the volatile time of returning to our home country.

The course materials heavily addressed the need to leave the host country well. We and another family we know had the unique privilege of attending DAR before the time we actually moved permanently away from the field. This was huge for us! When it was time for us to leave, we already had tools and coping strategies which made for a much smoother transition and helped us to leave well.

Having a time and a place to process the intense emotions of re-entry is invaluable, and I urge you to find a program you can be part of at all costs. You will not regret it, and it will be an incredible deposit into your emotional health as you move through the challenges of transition. Though you may have to fight feelings of guilt for spending money on yourself, believe me, the investment in a debriefing program is well worth it and very needed.

Maybe you are not a missionary or an expat, but you know one and love one and want to help them in their transition. First off, recognize that this is more than a physical move; it's an emotional one. Find ways to be sensitive to the nature of this move by asking the good, hard questions, by being available to fully listen (not fix or advise). Also, recognize when space is needed and remember that this is not a rejection of you or the new life that you are hoping your loved one will readily embrace and enjoy. It is a natural response to the grief, and they may need the space to process. A friend of mine who recently moved back to the United States says it this way, "It was difficult because our family and friends were so excited that we were back but we weren't excited to be back. We knew that God called us back, but we just weren't ready to be back."

I would also say to especially be intentional and understanding toward singles. I believe their re-entry is uniquely difficult because they are processing it alone. They don't have the benefit of a spouse as a sounding board, someone to comfort and understand them and go through the emotions of re-entry together.

Many of our close friends have had to brave the waters of transition alone, and it is incredibly hard. It is difficult when others don't understand, or when people forget to check in and solitude feels magnified. In any way possible, reach out to your single friend or family member on a regular basis with genuine questions and care. Draw them into conversations and don't assume that they are doing well with the transition process.

Preparing emotionally takes effort and time. But it is well worth it. It helps pave a smoother path to the other side. So take the time to enter in. Don't fight it; don't run from it. Surround yourself with excellent resources and people in order to navigate the emotions of re-entry well. Because it can be done.

In the next chapter I will discuss ideas on how to prepare kids well for the transition back to their home country. Oftentimes I believe young people can tend to be forgotten or disregarded during this process. Paying attention and being intentional can go a long way in helping kids make the transition smoothly.

Chapter 5
Preparing Our Kids

Many people assume that because kids are generally adaptable and resilient, they will do just fine in an international move, and there is little need to spend extra attention on them. Others go the opposite extreme and worry incessantly on how their children will do adjusting back to life in their passport country, a place they may not have lived in for many years. Either camp fails to recognize that children are capable of surviving re-entry given the proper tools and the nurturing from their parents.

Why is it so important to prepare our children well for life back in a home that was once theirs or perhaps has never been theirs? I believe and have seen first hand that how well you prepare your kids for re-entry will greatly determine how well they will go through it. It will also greatly affect the quality of your relationship and the connection you'll have with them at the time.

Re-entry done well for kids can pave the way for their adaptation to their new world and a healthy understanding of who they are in relation to their past world. Re-entry done poorly can greatly affect a child's identity and can carry with it many difficulties for them later on, one being unresolved grief. It is our opportunity and responsibility as parents to help our kids work through their grief. Remember, they are losing a home, friends, perhaps a school and beloved pets, a way of life they've grown accustomed to for many years.

It is vital to remember that our kids' experience of their host country can be vastly different from our own. As adults we *chose* to move there in the first place after probably having lived the majority of our lives in our home countries. Missionary and expatriate kids are a whole different story. They had little, if any, choice in the matter and may have been very young when they moved to the host country. Perhaps they were even born there. Their whole world and understanding of how life works is intricately bound up in their experience of their host country.

Speaking from the experience of a missionary kid, it is incredibly tough to go through re-entry. It literally feels like your world is being turned upside down. And not only that, but it feels like your insides are too. Your identity comes into question, and you're not sure what to hang onto for stability. More than anything else, the experience can feel lonely, like no one understands what you are going through.

I remember the summer I graduated from high school. Right after graduation my family moved away from Bolivia, my home ever since I was four years old. Though I was excited to start college, I was also processing grief and fear of the unknown. That summer we spent time at my uncle's lake house, surrounded by cousins and food and chatter. All I wanted to do was cry. And I didn't know why. I just felt strange, like I was in a place I was supposed to understand and be part of, but I felt so out of place. I was supposed to know these people and engage with them but I had only seen them off and on throughout my life. *Who was I? How could I be part of their world?*

I also remember the first few months of living in Chicago my freshman year of college. One day I had the urge to go to the roof of our ten-story dorm building and shout to the surrounding skyscrapers, the bustle of taxis and buses, the sounds of construction, the people commuting: "Can everyone just slow down and take a siesta?" Where we lived in Bolivia the city would literally shut down for two hours every single afternoon while people rested. No businesses would be open; all would take a break. This was the way of life I had been used to.

So, don't assume that your kids will be okay because they are naturally prone to be resilient and flexible. Keep in mind that no matter their age, they will still be going through the emotions and difficulty of transition.

Don't wait too long to tell them that you will be leaving the field and returning to your home country. Attempting to shield them from pain will only create more. Yes, young children struggle with an understanding of time, but there are ways you can help them understand the time frame whether it's doing paper chains or giving them a frame of reference like "after sister's birthday." Be honest with them from the beginning even if you fear an adverse reaction from them.

And be careful not to project your own experiences onto them. Their experience of their host country is unique, and their identities and personalities are still developing within the context of their overseas life; you can expect that their reaction to and understanding of this change will be different than yours. And that's okay.

Do focus on your relationships with your kids. Be intentional, especially during this volatile time, to continue building strong connections with each of them. The more you can create a sense of safety and stability within your family while changes abound all around your kids, the more protected and cared for they will feel. Recognize that each of them will undoubtedly display different reactions to the change going on around them. Affirm, listen to, and attempt to understand each one.

And remember, how you are reacting to the change directly affects them. I'm not saying that you should hide your emotions so they won't be sad or that you put up a false front in order to protect them. I'm saying pay attention to your own reactions, find ways to minimize stress, take care of yourself emotionally, and engage your kids in dialogue as you each process the upcoming life change.

A missionary who worked in Bolivia with my parents had great perspective on how to help older kids cope with the change. She said that letting kids have a part in making decisions and giving them a chance to explore their own solutions is really key. That way they maintain a sense of control when they are entering a season that is very tumultuous. She went on to say that they coped by having animals because pets are important.

Depending on the ages of children you have there are resources that can be helpful to their re-entry. My siblings and I greatly benefited from an MK summer camp put on by an organization called Interaction that specifically aimed to help MKs adjust back to life in the United States. Not only did the camp leaders help all of us clueless MKs learn how to write checks, keep a budget, go shopping, apply for a job, and tackle other practical life skills, they listened to our hearts and our stories. We found a place and a space to be understood, to be heard.

And probably best of all, we were gathered together with other MKs from around the world who shared similar experiences and to whom we could all relate. If you can find a place like this or get your college bound kid involved in an MK group on campus or connected with other MKs, this will go far to helping them feel supported and understood. I've already mentioned the Debriefing and Renewal program offered through MTI. They have an excellent kids' program for all ages in which they are intentional about helping these kids put words to their experience of re-entry, and they gift them with powerful tools to handle it well.

Our kids were very young when they left Nicaragua: almost 5, 3½ and almost 2. Besides our furlough year, living in Nicaragua was all that our 5 year old and 3 ½ year old knew. They were born there, learned to crawl and walk there, and didn't know anything different. Some might say "well, at least your two year old won't have a clue what is going on," but we chose to not underestimate the effect this move would have on all of our kids, including our youngest. We decided to be intentional with each of them and as a family. From the beginning we let them know that we would be moving away from Nicaragua, and we began preparing them for the change.

It's true that kids at that age have a hard time grasping a proper sense of time. Yesterday in their minds could have been last week, and tomorrow is Christmas already. So it was tempting not to let them in on this big life change until we were close to leaving. But we chose to involve them almost right away in the leaving process. We knew it would be difficult for them to understand that it was months away, but we believed in the benefits of preparing them well, no matter how young they were.

And so we engaged on their level. We explained why we were leaving Nicaragua (sometimes we had to tell them again and again). We made a chart together contrasting what they loved about Nicaragua (and would miss) against what they were excited about in Colorado. We regularly prayed for new friends in Colorado. Our kids helped us make a Venn diagram together where we listed out things that were different about each place and things that would remain the same (ex: Mommy and Daddy are with you, Jesus is with us, we get to go to school, we'll still play sports, etc).

We engaged their questions and always listened when they had something to say about leaving Nicaragua, even if it was in the form of a complaint. We validated their feelings and reinforced that it was normal for them to be feeling both sadness about leaving Nicaragua and excitement about moving to Colorado all at the same time.

We talked about our transition often, in the car, in our home, at bed times, when we were out and about. We read books like *The Leaving Morning* by Angela Johnson and talked about other friends who had moved on before us. We involved the kids in saying goodbye to their friends and teachers. They did this in tangible ways like picking out a treasured toy to pass on to them and drawing pictures and writing notes. They also had a special "last day of school" celebration at the Nicaraguan preschool they attended. These were all ways we were intentional about preparing our kids for the move.

There are hundreds of other ideas I'm sure, and the best part about being a family is the opportunity for creativity and making things personal. Luke and I also geared ourselves up for how the kids would react during re-entry, and we began praying early on that God would give us wisdom and awareness of kids' individual needs. We prepared ourselves by expecting that there would be varying kinds of reactions from potty training regressions to unexplainable meltdowns.

In whatever shape or form you choose to prepare your kids, the main thing is that you do it. I cannot emphasize enough how beneficial it is for them and ultimately for you to be well prepared. They will tangibly experience your love and care for them as they see you openly communicate about this change and intentionally help them navigate the emotions of leaving and entering. Kids are resilient, yes, but they need tools, resources and support just as adults do in order to survive re-entry and thrive in their new home.

Chapter 6
Letters to Nicaragua and Bella

One of the ways that I said goodbye to dear people in Nicaragua was through letter writing. It was a tangible way that I could thank them, honor them and process my own grief of saying goodbye. While I will not include letters to individuals here in this chapter, I am including a letter to Nicaragua and a letter to our beloved dog, Bella.

Dear Nicaragua,

It's hard to believe that in just four days we will be saying goodbye to you. And I don't know when we're coming back, whether for a visit or to live again.

I remember when I came for the first time so many years ago, and I didn't know a soul. I was young, excited, naive, and yet I thought I knew what you were like since I had grown up in Bolivia. I assumed things were similar, if not the same here.

I remember in my first few months here I experienced a daily flood of memories from my childhood. Thoughts I had kept locked away came back to me in full force. I remember struggling with these memories, experiencing nostalgia and trying to reconcile these thoughts from the past with my present-day, first experiences in Nicaragua. These buried memories hadn't had much relevance to my life in the States and did not get expressed much except to close friends I could trust.

Eventually, after those first few months, a distinction began to form, and I was able to separate my growing-up years in Bolivia and this new experience. You were different. I was different. I was no longer a child following my parents' calling, just doing what my family was doing. Now I was an adult making my own choices, deciding to enter your beautiful country and learn and grow and change and experience you.

I learned so much in those first few months. I quickly learned what words were offensive or didn't make sense here (I'm grateful that your people are gracious and forgiving). It seemed to take me forever to make the switch from automatically saying "Ciau" all the time to "Adios." Now it is the most natural thing ever, and it would be difficult for me to reverse that habit.

I remember back when everything was an adventure, a new and exciting experience. Before I even stepped foot on your soil, I was inexplicably drawn to you, intrigued by you. And now eleven years later, I can say with certainty you have become my home.

They say home is where the heart is. Pieces of my heart will always be here, in this place where I met my love, where I struggled through depression, where I experienced triumphs, joys, fruit, and where I experienced disappointment and despair. This place where our first two kids were born, where Luke and I made a home together, where we served alongside in ministry.

Your country will always have my heart for it was here I truly learned to live, to live free. Of guilt, shame, pressure to perform. It was here where I truly grew up. Thank you for sharing yourself with me, an outsider. Thank you for welcoming me. Thank you for giving me so many wonderful memories, for being part of my story.

I love the beauty of your land. I love that in many senses it is "undiscovered beauty" and has not become a tourist trap. I love your simplicity. Life is slower and things are laid back and not complicated (most of the time). I love your people. I have been amazed at their hospitality, more often than not expressed in an attitude of genuine openness and receptiveness to foreigners. I love that your people are gracious and forgiving when we blunder, when we mess up and offend. I love seeing your people celebrate and enjoy life and their families. You all have time for each other. You look out for each other and take great care of each other. I love that about the body of Christ here.

I'm sorry for the times I have criticized you, complained about you. For failing to see your beauty and potential, for not believing in change. I'm sorry for thinking I know all about you, that there's nothing left to learn. I'm sorry for letting my pride blind me at times to your strengths and instead, focusing on your weaknesses. I'm thankful again for your graciousness, for your hospitality not merely as I entered your country but throughout my time here. I'm thankful for your humility and understanding as I (and my kind) make these mistakes and hopefully learn from them.

I will miss you. Probably more than I realize right now. I will miss the comfort of this place, the safe haven it can seem to be from the social and political problems of the U.S. I will miss the delicious food, prepared with the intent of not only feeding physical bodies but fostering relationships and spending time together. I will miss speaking Spanish daily and interacting with your beautiful and unique people. I will miss experiencing the resourcefulness of your people. I will miss being able to hand my child to a stranger in a moment of need or crisis. I will miss being ushered to the front of the line at the bank because I am pregnant or have a baby with me (oh, how I love how your country values children!) And I will miss being surrounded by the reminders of the many precious memories I've made here. These are my "story places."

This is my prayer for you: that God would bless this land, not only financially but with peace, with strength and with transformation. May you fight for justice and take a stand against corruption. I pray you would hold on to what is true, what is good...it will liberate you. You have so much potential. Don't waste it. Keep welcoming, keep loving, keep developing, and keep valuing relationships. You are one of a kind, Nicaragua, and I am so grateful for the privilege of having lived here and having been shaped by your land and people. You will forever be in my heart. I look forward to the day when I see you again.

Much love and prayers,
Ellen

Dear Bella,

You have been a great dog to me, a faithful companion, a quiet and steady presence (except for when you are extremely hyper). You were like our first child. I remember when we first got you, and you were timid, especially around Luke. And now sometimes I think you almost prefer him over me. He will miss taking you on runs and walks. You were a great running companion.

I love how you are so good with our kids, so gentle yet protective of them. With each new baby added to the family, you welcomed them and were instantly on guard against any potential harm that could come to them. They will miss you so much (especially Lucy). What fun they had chasing you around the yard, giving you baths, playing with you at the beach and crawling all over you. We could not have asked for a gentler dog that was so good with kids.

We hate to leave you. You are part of our family, and we leave a piece of our hearts here in Nicaragua when we go. This time we are not coming back after a year away (but maybe to visit). We know you'll be sad and confused but please know that we love you even though we couldn't take you with us.

Your new owners will take good care of you. You know them. You will be safe. They will love you. Make new memories with them, trust them and know you are loved. Thank you for being a wonderful friend. I love you and will miss you, Bella.

Love,
Ellen

Action Points for
Part One: The Leaving

Chapter 1:

For missionaries* considering a move back to their home country:

1. Seek counsel from a trusted friend or mentor.
2. To aid in your decision process, make a pro's and con's list (be honest and leave no ideas out).
3. Take an all-day (or longer) retreat to spend some time thinking, praying, and seeking God.

For churches and organizations:

1. Clearly communicate expectations of time commitments from missionaries.
2. Be listening for signs of burnout and fatigue from missionaries; offer counsel and aim to stay involved in the decision-making process the missionary is going through.
3. Be proactive and take preventative measures to help counteract any possible negative reasons a missionary may leave the field.

4. Talk openly with the missionary throughout their time overseas about healthy and unhealthy reasons they may choose to return to their home country.

Chapter 2:

For missionaries:
1. Make a list of special people in your life.
2. Schedule intentional time with each of them with plenty of time before the stressful days leading up to your move.
3. Think of ways to express your gratitude toward close friends (either through letter writing or giving a gift or verbal affirmation) and then follow through.

For family, friends, and supporters:
1. Be genuinely interested in the special people who are in your missionary's life; show empathy toward them about having to say goodbye to special friends.
2. Encourage your missionary to say goodbye well.

Chapter 3:

For missionaries:
1. Make a list of favorite places and plan to visit them at least once before you leave.
2. Plan to have a get-away to a special spot before the stress of moving hits.
3. Organize your items for sale plenty of time in advance and decide how and when you will arrange for pick up and payment.
4. Involve your family in sharing treasured items with treasured friends.

5. Be sure to think of all the details you will need to take care of so that you won't be leaving unfinished business for others to take care of.

For family, friends, and supporters:
1. If possible, visit your missionary before they leave the field, take interest in those special places and show empathy toward your missionary as they say goodbye.
2. Be intentional to ask about how your missionary is dealing with saying goodbye to special places.

Chapter 4:

For missionaries:
1. Continue a habit of journaling or try it out.
2. Write your own Psalm of Lament.
3. Pick one of the recommended books to read.
4. Make a list of things you will miss about your host country; be specific about how that loss will affect you.
5. Pray over the above list, thanking God for the people and memories in your host country that are dear to you.
6. Remind yourself of your true identity by making a poster or sign with truths about who you are in Christ.
7. Schedule a debriefing time, preferably within the first six months that you are back.

For family, friends, and supporters:
1. Ask how your missionary is doing emotionally with the change ahead and truly listen.
2. Buy a book from the resource list and gift it to them.
3. Encourage a debriefing time; offer to pay for part or all of it.

For churches and organizations:
1. Buy a few books from the resource list and give them to your missionary when they return (they will not want extra things to pack).
2. Schedule and pay for a debriefing time; this will speak volumes of value to your missionary.
3. Follow up after the debriefing time; ask how it went, what things were learned and how you can continue to come alongside the missionary in their transition.

Chapter 5:

For missionaries:
1. Sign your kids up for a re-entry program or an MK summer camp.
2. Be intentional about goodbyes with your kids: plan a goodbye party for them, help them write notes to friends, encourage them to give a special toy to a friend they will miss.
3. Talk with your kids about the paradox of being sad about leaving their home and being excited about a new one...and that this is okay! Make a chart contrasting the old home to the new one.
4. Read *The Five Love Languages of Children* by Gary Chapman, determine which love languages each of your children has and be intentional about showing them that love before, during and after the move.

For family, friends, and supporters:
1. Gather resources for the kids and encourage a formal re-entry program.

2. Educate yourself on the challenges of being a third culture kid and find ways to empathize and relate to them.
3. Ask the kids honest questions about the host country and genuinely listen.

For churches and organizations:
1. Pay for a re-entry program or an MK summer camp.
2. Take genuine interest in the kids and find out how you can communicate love and support to them.

* I use the term "missionaries" because that was my context and my experience. However, these action steps apply to a broader range of people: expats, embassy workers, military, and global workers of any kind.

ELLEN ROSENBERGER

Part Two
The Chaos

"The only way to make sense out of change is to plunge into it, move with it, and join the dance."
- Alan W. Watts

Chapter 7
The Last Days

I've written about the leaving stage, and now we move into the chaos stage. This is not to say that this stage will most definitely feel chaotic, but it is definitely a period of time (anywhere from a few weeks to a few months) where it is most unsettling. It's the in-between stage. You have left or are about to leave your home and may not be quite settled into your new one. This stage is characterized by suitcases, travel, temporary housing, staying with relatives, finding housing, and everything that is transient.

Really, the chaos stage begins in those last few days in your host country. The days of finishing packing, moving out of your house, and preparing for your travels. The days of the final farewells and tying up loose ends and taking care of last-minute details.

Our family's last few days in Nicaragua were full and busy but thankfully not as stressful and anxiety-ridden as they probably could have been. Yes, we were packing and sorting and re-deciding on items that wouldn't fit in our suitcases. And yes, we were closing bank accounts and settling bills and selling the last of our household items. But in the midst of all the to-do's and the activity, we did not feel overwhelmed.

One thing that continued to help me feel grounded was journaling. Even in the midst of the chaos, I made the time to reflect and express gratitude as well as ask God to keep supplying peace in the midst of change. Here is a journal entry from several days before we left Nicaragua where I found expression for my thoughts.

June 20, 2016

Dear Jesus,

Thank You for music, for the way it lifts me, gives me life, energy, peace, pleasure. Thank You for quiet, for a start to the morning by myself. Thank You for Your eternal, true and holy Word. May it fill my heart and mind with truth all day long. Thank You for Your grace and mercy, Your kindness, Your patience, Your blessings (health, my family, safety, peace, provision, friendship). Would you please continue to give me endurance, strength, peace and confidence as we walk through this last week in Nicaragua? So much to do and so little time...please help me to get sleep, to not be stressed and irritated and to be disciplined so I'm not doing last-minute things....I really hate that! Please help me not to be overwhelmed at the tasks.

My heart is yours,
Ellen

I'm thankful we had a strange sense of peace and steadiness as we went through our last days. A comforting realization that we had been processing this impending loss all along and hadn't saved it for the last moments. Can you believe that we even took our kids to watch a movie the day before our plane boarded? We would not have been able to enjoy that fun, "beat-the-heat" family activity had we been running around in every direction. We were even able to enjoy time with a few family members who were in Nicaragua with a missions team from their church. This would not have happened if we were drowning in anxiety and busyness.

Luke and I attribute this ability to enjoy the last days with little stress to the effort and intentionality we consistently put into the leaving stage. Leaving well not only helps you re-enter well, but I believe it can help you handle the potential stress of the chaos stage well. No matter how many stories you have heard of others being incredibly overwhelmed during the chaos stage, that does not mean that has to be your story. Plenty of our friends have experienced high anxiety during the last days in country, and this was paralyzing to them in terms of making decisions about what items were packed or left behind. Others were frantically leaving behind underwear and random items even on the way to the airport.

I'm not saying you can eliminate stress completely. There will be aspects of this time that are characterized by stress, and you will probably feel yourself running on adrenaline for a lot of it. But the more you can prepare yourself before this stage hits, the better.

So, plan ahead. Do everything you can do to prevent last-minute stress. Logistics matter. Even down to how and when you sell your household items, where you will stay the last few days, who will take you to the airport and who you will spend your time with.

Accomplishing all the nitty gritty details of moving is not only helpful for you, it's helpful for your community, those who are left behind. What kind of wake will you leave in your path? One that is subtle and calm or a big one, one that requires others to clean up after you? Do you want to leave behind good and positive memories of your presence in that country or a negative last impression because of unfinished business and details left for others to take care of.

I recognize there are often extenuating circumstances and situations of emergencies that require missionaries to rely on the grace and help of others to sell their things, move their stuff, take care of their vehicles, etc, but if at all possible be sure to plan ahead and take care of your responsibilities. You will honor others by respecting their time and energy.

Amy Young talks about this at length in her book *Looming Transitions*. She describes people as either pre-grievers or post-grievers. Pre-grievers are those who are intentional about processing their grief even before they leave while post-grievers are not going through the grieving process until after they leave. I believe we were able to reduce stress in those last days by having already put the mental energy toward grieving, toward saying goodbye. When the time came for the final goodbyes, we felt prepared for them, like we had been prepping for them all along. This reduced the stress and anxiety of any thoughts such as "Oh wait! I'm not ready for this!" or "I wish I had said goodbye to that place or that person! Now I don't have the time!"

Something else that helped us handle the last days well was the big and small ways that our community pitched in. The day we were supposed to move out of our house (a few days before our flight) I got a message from a friend. Not a close friend, not even a friend that I saw frequently. But she asked me how I was handling the moving and if there was anything she could help with. My first thought was "Yes! Would you take my one and a half year old off my hands for a few hours so I can actually finish packing without her getting into one more suitcase?"

I almost didn't ask, but I reminded myself that we need other people and she was offering. She was more than happy to have Lucy for the morning, and I was able to finish moving out of our house kid-free. So, don't be afraid to ask for help. You're going to need it, and people are generally willing to lend a hand. They won't know how they can help if you don't tell them.

We were blessed beyond measure to be able to stay our last two nights with a missionary couple whom we had known the whole

72

time we were in Nicaragua. They had played influential roles in our lives, and we had made many wonderful memories with their family. They were the couple who led us through premarital counseling, and we had mentored their kids through youth group.

It was comforting to be able to stay in their home our last two nights in Nicaragua. These were people who were incredibly special to us and knew us well. Their hospitality meant the world to us. Not only did they provide a place for us to sleep and eat and end our chapter of life in Nicaragua, but they were intentional to have conversations with us and send us off in prayer. They invited over a number of our closest friends for final goodbyes on the last night. They even had prepared little airplane bags for the kids, filled with snacks and activities for the flights. These small actions of kindness had a huge impact on us.

The emotions of these last days were a mix and a blur. I'm thankful I did not have stress and anxiety clouding them. What I did feel more than anything else was a bit of a numbness. A sense of "Is this really happening?" *All this preparation and planning and anticipation and now what? We're just going to step on a plane and leave? How can this be?*

It didn't feel real when we pulled away from our house. It didn't feel real when we said goodbye to our beloved dog, Bella. It didn't feel real when we said those last goodbyes.

Hadn't we always been the ones being left? And now we were the ones leaving. I knew how to be the one being left. I didn't know how to be the one leaving. It didn't feel real when we went to bed that last night knowing we would wake up to alarms proclaiming "this is departure day." It didn't feel real that we were leaving this country that we loved and that we would be arriving in the U.S. in a few short hours. But I knew it was.

This was really happening and though it felt strange, I had to walk through it knowing and believing that God was going to be by my side. He was going before us as we braved this new journey.

Through all the stages of leaving I kept communicating to others, expressing in big and small ways what we were going through. Below is a blog I wrote just hours before leaving Nicaragua.

June 24, 2016, Blog "24 Hours Left in Nicaragua"

In 24 hours we will be on an airplane headed to a different world. We'll say goodbye to Nicaragua, our home of twelve years, and in a few weeks say hello to a new one in Littleton, Colorado.

In case you hadn't heard, our family is moving to Colorado where Luke will be studying at Denver Seminary. He will begin a three-year program to earn a Master of Divinity in Youth and Family Ministries and hopes to use his degree in a pastoral capacity in the future (whether youth, associate, missions or other).

We would love your prayers for:
- *Safety in travel (we're flying to Indiana and then driving to Colorado)*
- *Smooth and healthy transition for us all*
- *Provision for our family*

Praise God for:
- *Sweet goodbyes with special people and places*
- *Peace amidst sadness of leaving this country we love*
- *His faithfulness and goodness*

Thank you for keeping us in your prayers!
Luke and Ellen Rosenberger

What will the last days be like for you? Will they be filled with stress and anxiety, endless tasks and overcrowded schedules? Or will you be able to pay attention as you say those final goodbyes? Will you truly notice the people you are leaving behind?

I can guarantee you the effort you put into "leaving well" will directly have an effect on your stress levels in those last days. It doesn't have to be chaotic or overwhelming. It could be sweet and full of closure. For me it felt numbing which I took to be normal. Whatever it is like for you, may you brave those last days with courage and strength as you walk toward the unknown.

Chapter 8
Entering The Chaos

From June 23rd to August 15th, 2016 our family did not have our own home to live in. In five weeks we were in two countries, nine states, five airports and slept in fifteen different places.

We had moved out of our house in Nicaragua on June 23rd and stayed at our good friends' house for our last two nights in Nicaragua. From there we had flown to Chicago and stayed with Luke's sister for three nights. During our stay we enjoyed time with Luke's sister, brother-in-law and our young nephew while fitting in a time to see good friends and supporters in the area. I took one night to squeeze in a short visit with my best college girlfriends.

Below is a journal entry I wrote the first morning we were back in the States. These thoughts were actually written on post-it notes because I could not find any paper (if that tells you anything about the nature of the chaos stage).

June 26, 2016

Woke up in a different world. Feels strange, disorienting, weird, unreal. How is it possible that yesterday morning we woke up in Managua, Nicaragua? Did all of this really happen? Did we just up and leave our home? Did all that prepping, planning, packing, moving, saying goodbyes really happen? Cuz all of the sudden here we are and all of that is instantly in the past. And I can feel my brain trying to reconcile it all. To fit my two worlds together...to make it all make sense. We spent so much time and energy on preparing for this transition and now here we are. Now what? How will we continue the transition on this side of things? What will life be like here? Will I be able to make the switch in my brain to this different place? It is familiar, I know it, I've lived in it before but how will I be able to now enter as one truly living here (gulp) permanently? How will I be able to let go of the past and my old home and live in the new one? What do I do with the memories of my old home? Who will care about them? Who will ask about them? Who will listen? Who will understand? This is day 1 of transitioning on the other side now. Ready or not. I know we did all we could to prepare, to be intentional about goodbyes to people and places. I have to believe that will help on this end. It feels a little like I'm thrown into this transition, like I'm being tossed by the waves. What if I didn't feel ready? I would still be here. I almost feel at the mercy of this transition. How will I react? How will I handle it? Will I sink or swim? How many lives do I get? Can I drown one day but wake up the next with a new set of lungs and a resolve to try again? Will I get stronger and have more energy and strategies to fight the waves? Or do I just roll with the waves like they tell you to do if you ever get caught in a riptide? Will I weather this transition with my family members or will we be pulled in all different directions unable to hear each other because of the waves, fighting this thing on our own? I guess I'll find out. Hopefully I survive and even do well.

After spending our first few days in the States with Luke's sister, we then proceeded to where most of Luke's other family members live. We stayed with a different sister for six nights. This was our week of seeing family, visiting Luke's parents' church, and getting an incredible amount of tasks accomplished at the same time. Luke had to get license plates and insurance for the cars we would be driving down to Colorado. We had family events to attend and a former small group to meet up with. It was a whirlwind of a week. Enjoyable yes, but full and busy especially with the added responsibilities that had to be taken care of before our road trip to Colorado.

Here is a journal entry I wrote during that week as I reflected on our transition and how each of our kids seemed to be processing this change.

June 30, 2016

It's Day 6 in the United States. It feels a bit like a whirlwind but thankfully I have not felt overwhelmed. I believe it's still the prayers of many people carrying us during our preparation, travel and now transition. I guess I just keep taking it one day at a time and I'm not stressed. But shouldn't I be? The kids are doing great. David is loving being reunited with his best bud and cousin. He has not mentioned Nicaragua very much or his friends there. Perhaps once the vacation-feel of our time in the States wears off he'll start thinking more about Nicaragua. He's doing pretty well behavior-wise and is being flexible and going with the flow. Emily has reverted to almost 100% Spanish. It is so fascinating. I engage her in it and am happy to keep her speaking it. Interesting way she is coping with the change I believe. We never really spoke Spanish at home.

79

She's been a bit testy, hyper, clingy, and generally "off" a bit. Lucy has done wonderfully. Aside from crying a bit our last few nights in Nicaragua, she has done so well. I expected her to be really clingy, to suck her thumb even more than normal and to be constantly saying "Bella." But she has done none of these things. She is so chill, so happy, flexible, just goes with the flow. I think she's doing well because she knows she's loved and is with her family. It makes me a little sad that she isn't saying "Bella" (it's like she's instantly forgotten). Maybe all the change during our week of moving was what was making her extra clingy and thumb sucking and now that we're not in that anymore she's fine? I've been doing okay...don't think about it too much (not on purpose). Just focusing on enjoying the family and activities. I guess I'm resting my brain from all the flurry of activity leading up to leaving - all the packing, planning, etc. I'm excited, really excited about Colorado. I hope I'm not placing too many expectations (or too high of expectations) on it and that we will not be disappointed. I feel a bit numb at this stage right now...is it because it hasn't hit me yet? When will it hit me? When will it be hard? I don't think I'm pushing it away or avoiding it...just am not thinking about it too much.

On our way to Colorado we made a one night stop in Kansas City to spend the 4th of July with my brother and sister-in-law. We then spent the next two nights in Oklahoma City with good friends whom we had known from Nicaragua. They had moved back to the States almost a year prior.

Here is a journal entry I wrote during our visit with these good friends that highlights how I processed seeing them in their new life in the States.

July 7, 2016

It feels so strange to be around our friends....almost like we were friends in a different world and that world doesn't exist so does our friendship still exist? It's weird seeing them settled here, with a new house, new car, new baby....I'm just not used to it...it's hard to process it all at once...and it's like they've "moved on", assimilated, re-joined this culture all of the sudden but I have to remind myself that they've been here for almost a year already, this process has taken time (but I haven't been here to see it). What will our friendship look like up here? Will it just slowly fade, will it feel awkward, stay the same, grow? Being here feels a little like grieving...seeing their new home/new life...it's all in-your-face evidence that our times in Nica and our friendship in Nica is long over. This is the new normal and we will never have that again. Feels sad and strange. Do they miss it? Do they sometimes want to go back or wish it was like it used to be? This is reality now, like it or not. It's different and will take getting used to.

As we got closer to our destination in Colorado, I thought more about leaving Nicaragua and the following journal entry reflects on the thoughts going through my mind at that time.

July 8, 2016

I miss our house. Crazy to think that we moved out two weeks ago yesterday. I can still picture it - both set-up and empty in those last days. Maybe I should email our landlady. Can't believe we forgot to empty our junk drawer! I will miss the peacefulness, the privacy of our home. Was it really only two weeks ago that we lived there? And we won't live there again

- weird. I'm sure it will feel strange to visit someday. Today we make it to Castle Rock (our home for the month of July). I'm ready to be settled somewhere though we jump around a bit in July.

One more night on the road (a random motel in Dalhart, Texas), and we were finally at our semi-permanent destination of Castle Rock, Colorado where we would spend the next five weeks living at yes, another of Luke's sisters' homes. However, our family would be living there on our own since her family was out of state for a few months due to her husband's job.

Here are a few journal entries I wrote upon our arrival to Colorado as the reality of our move here began to set in, and I processed through what it would be like to start settling in.

July 9, 2016

We made it to Colorado! It feels so great to be here! Luke said as we pulled into his sister's house: "It feels good to be somewhere". After almost two weeks of travel I agree. It was a beautiful drive from Texas through New Mexico and to Colorado. The sign said "Welcome to Colorful Colorado" and it very much is. Really looking forward to living in this beautiful, beautiful state. When we got to my sister-in-law's house, we felt immediately welcomed to Colorado by my aunt. She had left gifts, food, cleaning supplies and toilet paper for us! She's so thoughtful and we felt so welcomed. Some of my thoughts once we finally made it here: Are we crazy? What are we thinking? Coming here with no jobs, three kids, school bills to pay and fully knowing there would be a high cost of living. What? Is this unwise? What are "normal" people thinking? But I have to believe that God will provide those jobs, that money to live on and to pay schooling and the peace that He goes before us and is with us. That we are not crazy. That it's not crazy to trust in His provision in His timing. That all will be okay. No need to panic or freak out. Just take it one day at a time, one task at a time: find jobs, find furnishings, get involved at a church, find schools for kids, figure out schedules. All will come with time and there is time.

July 10, 2016

Yesterday we woke up excited about garage sales! Our first day in Castle Rock and we hit the garage sales right away! Found some amazing deals. I felt a little down in the afternoon...like alone. Here we are in a neighborhood we don't know, in a house not ours....who were we? It was a strange feeling. Thankfully that feeling subsided later on. We unpacked our clothes and put them in drawers. That helped a lot I think with feeling more settled and not having to rummage through bags to find stuff. Need to keep giving myself a pep talk that things take time. I can't expect myself after almost twelve years abroad to just jump in and know how things work here and fit in and know everything. I will make mistakes and struggle and that's normal and okay. I need to give myself a break and some grace. I'm doing great. We're doing well. Keep going.

Though we were semi-settled in Castle Rock, there was still a lot of movement and transiency to our life. During the five weeks of living in Castle Rock I would go on a Thrive retreat for global women, and Luke and I would travel to Los Angeles for his brother's wedding.

In the journal entries below I write about the Thrive Retreat and the impact it had on me in this transition. The ministry of Thrive hosts retreats in several different countries each year to give a place of rest, refreshment, and care for global women. The one I attended was specifically for those who are on a furlough or have come back to live in the States.

July 13, 2016

I'm at the Thrive Retreat. I've only been here for 24 hours and it is excellent! I feel so pampered and cared for and listened to. I've enjoyed meeting new people and was surprised to see an old friend from Moody Bible Institute! I love how everything is intentional and organized. That speaks value. I don't have to be the one to plan it or be frustrated by organizing it. It is done excellently with an emphasis on prayer and small groups with a recognition that we come from all walks of life and situations that brought us Stateside. There is freedom to spend our free time however we want. I'm so grateful to those who have made this retreat possible. It is an incredible blessing! I feel blessed beyond belief. I (and others) were in tears when the retreat leaders told us about the Boutique where we could go "shopping" (for free) for clothes and books! New clothes with tags on them! And the retreat coordinator said they rejected any donations of hand-me-downs! Wow.

July 16, 2016

Just got back from the Thrive Retreat yesterday. It was EXCELLENT! So organized, intentional, relaxing, encouraging. I loved every minute of it and it went by too quickly. At each station (hair cut, pedicure, massage) the women prayed for me! I loved the emphasis on prayer and that we spent time the last day in prayer for our small group members. They had gifts at our tables each morning (books, CDs, scripture coloring books) and the team delighted in lavishing these on us! I'm so thankful for the opportunity and would love to see many of my friends to go to Thrive and I want to support their ministry somehow.

Here is a journal entry I wrote after our trip to Los Angeles for Luke's brother's wedding and how Colorado was starting to feel like home.

July 25, 2016

One month ago today we were boarding a plane to leave Nicaragua. Feels strange....has it already been a month? And yet it feels like a long time ago at the same time. When we landed in Denver today the flight attendant said, "If Denver is your home, welcome home." Luke and I looked at each other. It is now. I'm excited about being in our new home. I loved flying back here. It felt right, good. Like it will make a good home. I'm getting anxious, excited, ready for our "new normal" to start kicking in.

These were my thoughts and emotions during all the chaos of traveling and the unsettledness we experienced. In the next chapter I'll describe how our family handled the chaos stage.

ELLEN ROSENBERGER

Chapter 9
How We Handled The Chaos Stage

The whole chaos stage was characterized by living out of suitcases, juggling where kids were going to sleep, trying to find that toothbrush or favorite stuffed animal or piece of paper to write something down. Our chaos stage didn't truly come to an end until we moved into our on-campus apartment at Denver Seminary on August 15th. And even then it took several weeks to get fully moved in and settled. To find everything and find a place for everything.

So, how did Luke and I handle this chaos stage? Probably the best way to describe it would be we stuck together. We braved it together like two people huddling under the same umbrella. We talked through our responses to a different culture, we reflected on how we were doing, we laughed at our floundering attempts to enter back into this life. This life we had never really lived in as a couple to begin with.

We shared common culture-shock experiences like having to resist the urge to give a little beep of the horn while driving. This was a common way in Nicaragua to give a friendly alert to other drivers that you were coming alongside them in the next lane, but here it would be taken as offensive.

Or the way we found ourselves feeling grateful to other people for the common courtesy of opening a convenience store door. We realized why this felt strangely kind to us: in Nicaragua almost all establishments had a paid armed guard standing at the door, and part of his job was to open the door for people. So when others did this out of their sheer goodwill, we were taken aback.

Or how we went crazy on our first day of garage saling. We found such incredible deals that we felt we couldn't pass up, including an all-white dining room table and chair set from IKEA for only $30. Later on we couldn't believe what we had been thinking! White chairs and a white table for our family with three spaghetti-spilling, accident-prone little kids? Maybe in our dreams or once we were empty nesters which did not feel like would come anytime soon, ha!

Or the strange feeling we would get when we walked in and out of a store, and no one was there to check our bags to make sure we weren't stealing anything. It felt almost wrong to be so trusted. I almost wanted to verbally let the store owners know "See I'm not stealing anything."

Or the weird sense we would get when we'd be in a neighborhood and not everyone would have a fence around their yard. It seemed so open, so unprotected. We were so used to homes in Nicaragua being surrounded by high walls and barbed wire. And yet the irony was not lost on us. Absence of fences yet seemingly little friendliness and openness to relationships. Physical barriers of walls and yet open homes and open hearts for friendships.

Also notable during this chaotic stage was the volatile emotional climate we were entering in the United States. The journal entry below expresses my response to our new environment.

July 9, 2016

It feels like we are coming into a broken, desperate, divided, frustrated country. The police shootings in Dallas, the Facebook wars, arguments over #blacklivesmatter, anger, violence, grief. All of it feels sobering. What is this country? Where are they (we?) headed?

We had to realize that not only were we different people than when we had left, but we were coming back to a different United States. Life is not static, and culture, values, and structures are constantly moving.

The emotional climate felt fragile, like a glass dish that was slipping from the counter onto unforgiving tile or perhaps had already broken on the floor. And who was picking up the pieces? We felt like we had stepped into a country that was torn by political tension and arguments over jargon and beliefs and policies and positions.

And growing under it all like a scratchy patch of grass was this increasing sense of frustration. This mentality that "I'm done with this country and these problems; let's just move to another country." Here we were entering back into this country and at the same time it seemed that many wanted to leave. We felt a tangible sense of disgruntledness along with "hands-in-the-air" attitudes.

Our hearts responded in sadness, turning to prayer, reflecting often on where this country was at and where it was headed. We had sensed the political tension from afar, but now it was a different feel to be part of this pivotal time in our country's history.

During this time we drew in as a family a lot, sticking to ourselves to provide constancy and a place of normalcy. We cautiously entered the surrounding culture, especially grocery stores and any place that would be anywhere remotely overwhelming for the eyes and mind. The journal below gives you a picture of the fear I had of going into a major grocery store.

July 12, 2016

On the way home yesterday we needed four grocery items and I didn't want to brave Walmart so we searched for a grocery store on the way. Ended up going to Tony's Market. A specialty, gourmet, organic shop. Felt so out of place. Grabbed my expensive items and got out!

It wasn't until I had been in the States for at least three weeks that I finally stepped into a grocery store. And it was with a friend of ours who had lived in Nicaragua but now had been back in the States for several years. She knew exactly what it felt like to be overwhelmed by the endless aisles of cereal and the way you could spend a half an hour comparing prices on one product alone. I was so grateful for her presence as we moved through the store with my list, and she helped me find each item one at a time all the while speaking encouraging words like "See, you're doing it!" and "Good job!" and "Okay, don't look at that, come over here, you got it, okay good." We even took a selfie to document our success, and we chuckled at the expressions of people passing us by.

This all might sound silly, but it's true. A good friend of mine who moved back to the States a year before us, literally threw up in Best Buy because she was so overwhelmed by all of the choices and bright lights and ads in the TV section. Sometimes seemingly easy and insignificant tasks can be overwhelming for those of us going through re-entry.

How did our kids handle this chaos stage? Phenomenally, actually. We did see a few evidences of their reaction to the change. They were a bit more clingy, whiny, and had increased misbehavior, which we were fully expecting. Emily had a few weeks of potty training regression, and we just decided to revert back to diapers and not continue to fight.

But on the whole they handled this huge life change like pros. We attribute this to the effort we put into preparing them well. They knew what was coming, and they were ready for it. We were intentional about reaffirming our love and care for them during all the upheaval of their world. Grounding them in the safety and comfort of our family was key for them surviving this chaos phase.

I also believe that kids pick up on how their parents are handling the stress of moving, and so as they saw Luke and I being stable, they were free to enjoy the adventure as well. Throughout this time we continued to freely encourage questions and comments about our life in Nicaragua and our new life in the States. We prayed together regularly as a family and were sure to point out when those prayers were answered (for new friends, a good school, etc).

Yes, it was difficult at times to keep everyone's stuff together as we traveled around and to find ways for the kids to expel their energy. Let's be honest; it's not ever really fun traveling with kids. It's a lot of work. But all in all, our family handled it well because we were prepared and because we strengthened our ties to each other.

What, on the practical level, helped us cope with all the unsettledness of the chaos stage? Continuing to talk together and reflect personally through journaling. Keeping in touch with friends and coworkers we had left behind whether it was a quick email or even a phone call. Being a learner and having a sense of adventure. Just as we had entered our host country all those years ago seeking to learn and understand and be part of the culture, we decided to do the same thing here. While all along giving ourselves grace and engaging in the gift of laughter.

It was helpful to maintain an attitude of flexibility, especially as certain plans didn't turn out exactly as we had envisioned them. All the months of preparation are helpful but many times once you get to the other side, it looks differently than you expected. A job may fall through, housing might not work out, or any number of situations may surface. We found out we were expecting our fourth child during the chaos stage! This was an opportunity to trust God with the details of our lives and the plans we had in mind.

During this time we had the unique privilege of seeing a large number of good friends from our life in Nicaragua. Either we traveled through their area of the country or they came through Colorado. It was a wonderful time to catch up with each of them, and our time together served sort of as a bridge from our old life to the new, cushioning the landing so to speak.

I don't know what the chaos stage will look like for you. Maybe you'll be like many of my friends and be in tears at grocery stores or in crowds of people. It could very well be a smooth though busy and full landing.

Whatever your experience has been or will be, I hope you will find the tools that will help you and your family brave it well. I hope you will prepare well and maintain attitudes of thankfulness and grace throughout the journey. This chaos season will end, and you will reach the end goal of settling. But it will take time, empathy, and determination. But you will get there.

Chapter 10
Letters to Self, Re-entry, and Colorado

As a window into my processing of a new environment, here I include letters to myself, to re-entry, and to Colorado. These are places where I could express my thoughts and emotions during the transition to my new home.

Dear Self,

I think you need a pep talk. Otherwise you might get caught in a trap of being way too hard on yourself. You need to remember that this moving thing, this transition thing is hard. And it's okay if you flounder a bit. It's actually okay if you sink a bit. If you didn't, you'd be superhuman. Don't forget that moving is one of the top five stressors in a person's life, right up there with a divorce or death of a family member. And that's just moving, not to mention moving internationally.

So breathe, laugh, cry, let it out, you're okay. This numb feeling, this uncertainty of knowing quite what to do with yourself, your thoughts and emotions are normal. Be kind to yourself. What you are going through is not easy. So cut yourself a break. Nobody but you can do that for yourself. If you don't give yourself some empathy, you will end up criticizing, expecting too much of and burdening yourself. Be willing to receive empathy and understanding. You need to believe it's okay to flounder, to struggle, to fail, to not get it all. You need to take a step back and smile or laugh.

Don't take this so seriously. You won't be perfect at this and that's perfectly fine. Give yourself grace and time. There is no rush. Don't expect so much of yourself. You've been through a lot. It's okay to do the bare minimum and be in survival mode for a while. No one will fault you. You don't need to prove anything to anyone else or to yourself.

Keep moving forward one step at a time, one day at a time, one moment at a time. You've got this. Don't be embarrassed, don't feel foolish. You are of more value and importance than your performance and ability to handle all of this reverse culture shock. You are more than just someone braving the waters of this transition. Your worth is not tied to how well you survive this change. Walk in confidence because you are loved, because you are known and because no matter what happens in this scary and unknown time of change, you know that you belong to Christ. He is with you and has gone before you. He is not far; He is near. Look to Him for your worth and for your help.

Dear Re-entry,

I sure don't like you very much. Sometimes not at all. You're difficult, uncomfortable, hard to live with and a lot of times hard to understand. And even though we've known each other for a long time now, I still don't like you very much. Yes, over the years I've gotten more and more used to your ways, but it doesn't necessarily make it easier or more pleasant. I'm sorry to say this, but you're just not very fun sometimes. Many times I find myself trying to ignore you or minimize your impact.

How come you can be so hard on some people? On the people I love and cherish? I hate seeing them struggle and grasp for solid ground like a leaf being swirled around helplessly in a windstorm. Why can going through you be so challenging? I wish there was a magic formula or strategy for handling you better. Tell me what it is if you know it. Why do I have to go through you to finally feel settled in my new land? Isn't there any other easier, less awkward way? When will this initial chaos stage be over? When will I not be overwhelmed at even the thought of stepping into a grocery store? When will I feel like I have arrived, like I'm normal, like one of the other human beings living in this place?

Even amidst my questions and my general dislike of you, I am thankful for the many ways I've grown because of you. I've learned to rely on Jesus, who knows me through and through and who is by my side in every change. He is the One who fully understands what it's like to go through you. I'm thankful that I've learned flexibility and helpful coping tools. I would not be able to handle you without those. I've learned a lot about myself, how I think, and how I process things. So, thank you for what you've taught me even if it's been in a not-so-pleasant way.

Re-entry, would you be kind to me and my family? Please don't take too long. Yes, do your work but remember to shape us, not break us. And go easy on those who are coming after us, okay?

Dear Colorado,

I'm in love. In love with your beauty. The fresh air. The breathtaking views of mountain tops touching cloudless skies. The sun beaming down, making all feel it's warmth and comfort. The lakes and rivers displaying peace. I love all of it. And I love how most of all, your natural beauty showcases the Creator's power and glory. Every day.

It is no wonder you are known as Colorful Colorado and people who move here usually stay here. Why wouldn't they? It is absolutely gorgeous in your state. Besides the views that are amazing, I love your weather. After living in a country where I'm dripping sweat even while just sitting in front of a fan, your low to no humidity is very much welcome! Not having to take multiple showers a day has been incredible. And what an added bonus that in the wintertime even the sun shines most days! What good news for this "can't-handle-gray-skies-all winter-long" girl!

I'm so excited to begin a fresh start here, to create our home here even if it's only for a few years. I'm thrilled that there are a ton of activities for our young kids. From playgrounds to libraries to parks. All free and easily accessible. Amazing! I am so excited about many free family and community events! It's wonderful that people are generally active here and get outdoors often. And of course my kids love to see dogs out and about virtually everywhere.

I wonder, do your people take your loveliness for granted? When they are driving to work or school do they still see, truly see the mountains? Or have these majestic beauties become a familiar backdrop? Will I ever take your incredible landscape for granted? Will this wonder wear off for me? Will this honeymoon stage of entering your land subside? When will living in you feel natural, normal, and old hat? How long will it take me to adapt to how your people live and go about their days?

Colorado, you are a new place for me. I'm excited to learn and grow in you. I'm excited for many new adventures. But I want you to know that even though I'm looking forward to living here, part of my heart is still miles away in a place very different. And that makes me different. I know I won't ever be a full, home-grown Coloradan. I will be one of those transplants. But I hope to be a transplant that brings perspective and life and a different view.

I hope you will open your eyes to what you have here in this unique piece of the globe and that you will be aware of what is outside your state lines. What other beauty exists. What other pain exists. That you would open your eyes to a greater world and be open to being influenced by it. I'm thankful for the journey of doing life in your beautiful land, learning from you, being part of you, being shaped by you, and hopefully influencing you as well.

ELLEN ROSENBERGER

Action Points for
Part Two: The Chaos

Chapter 7:

For missionaries*:

1. How would you describe what a peaceful last few days in country looks to you? What action steps do you need to take now to achieve this goal?
2. If necessary or desired, ask a close friend in advance if you can stay with them your last few nights in your host country.
3. Decide ahead of time where you will spend your energy in the final days.

For family, friends, and supporters:

1. Don't expect a lot of communication during these days; the best thing you can do is pray for low stress and smooth last days.
2. Don't ask a lot of questions that require decision making (such as where should we eat for dinner after we pick you up from the airport).

Chapter 9:

For missionaries:

1. Read or reference re-entry materials.
2. Choose to laugh about and share stories of reverse culture shock with others.
3. Don't expect too much out of yourself or your family members during this stage.
4. Continue journaling and trust that the settling stage will come.

For family, friends, and supporters:

1. Ask the hard questions and be willing to listen.
2. Don't be offended or make fun of your missionary if they make a cultural blunder or don't know what something is.
3. Be a shoulder to cry on, offer a listening ear, and be available for prayer.

For churches and organizations:

1. Check in periodically, preferably in person or over the phone.
2. Offer practical help with moving, meeting furnishing needs, finding employment, etc.
3. Educate yourselves on the stages of transition and seek to be empathetic and a support to the missionary.

* I use the term "missionaries" because that was my context and my experience. However, these action points apply to a broader range of people: expats, embassy workers, military, and global workers of any kind.

Part Three
The Settling

"As you move outside of your comfort zone, what was once the unknown and frightening becomes your new normal."

- Robin S. Sharma

Chapter 11
What's Helped

The settling stage. Such an ambiguous time period. For some this feels like it takes years while for others it seems to happen pretty quickly. I think there are many different factors that influence how the settling stage goes. Are you returning to your home town? Do you have a house still? Are you going to be around family, a home church, a familiar area? How often did you come back on a furlough or for short visits?

For us, our settling stage was directly impacted by the fact that we had taken an eleven-month furlough shortly before our permanent move back. Our extended period of time to adjust to the culture of the United States really contributed to our success in settling when we returned, even though it was to a different state. We set up a home, established routines as a family, and figured out how to live in this country.

A healthy departure definitely paved the way for a smooth settling stage. Because we had properly processed goodbyes, taken care of any conflict, we were able to move on unhindered. We did not have unresolved issues or things hanging over our heads or lingering in our brains. Luke and I were able to focus on our new stage of life without regrets and distractions from our old one.

I believe that having a sense of adventure has greatly helped us in this settling stage. We approached this new season much like we had when we entered the mission field when all was new, and we were discovering so many aspects of the culture, how to get around and how things work. We enjoyed learning our way around Littleton, finding free and family-friendly community events to explore. We were curious and wanted to know the history of our new home.

We kept a sense of humor throughout this time, not being too hard on ourselves. I remember one time a few months after we moved here I was at the grocery store and had asked a new friend what I could pick up for her since she was sick with a stomach issue. She asked me to get Vernor's for her. I thought "Okay, sure I can get that" assuming it was a medicine. I walk up to the pharmacy counter and ask for Vernor's. The lady just looks at me like I'm crazy and says she's never heard of that before. Embarrassed I snuck away to a nearby aisle where I could privately ask Google. Little did I know that Vernor's is a brand of ginger ale! I still laugh when I think about asking a pharmacist for ginger ale!

Finding a community right away has been huge for our adjustment back. Before leaving Nicaragua, we began praying for a community of believers to be involved in and friends to share life with. And we began searching for that even before arriving in Colorado. It's amazing the privilege we have with the internet these days. We were able to watch sermons, read about the history and beliefs of our church, begin to apply for internships with the young adult ministry at our church all before saying goodbye to Nicaragua. Having a body we were already looking forward to joining really grounded us. We were able to enter in right away and not feel lost and unsure of where we fit. I know many of our friends who have really struggled to find their place, to find a community they can enter into. Not having this structure and safety net is so difficult during the settling stage.

We knew we would be entering a small and unique community at Denver Seminary. At first I did not want to live on campus because it seemed to me that we would be pretending to be college students again. How could we do that with young kids in an apartment complex? Plus, no pets were allowed, and so we'd have to leave our Bella. But as we explored our options we came full circle and decided that living on campus, at least for the first year, would be a wise decision. Yes, there were adjustments in how our family was used to living. Less privacy, no more allowing the kids to freely roam and play indoors and outdoors throughout the day. But the benefit of living with and near people of like values, goals, stage in life far outweighed anything else. To feel like we are all in the same boat is a great comfort.

I've found the seminary community to have a lot of similarities to the missionary community. Both are transient by nature, rely heavily on each other for help with childcare, a missing dinner ingredient, moving. Both share resources and empathy for common struggles. I couldn't help but think when we first moved here how it must feel to be a second or third year student and see another influx of new students and new families moving on campus in the fall. *Will they open their hearts and lives to us even as they still grieve other families that have graduated and moved on?*

We chose to jump right into our communities and get involved. Though we were careful not to overcommit our schedules especially since this was the first semester of seminary for Luke, we did not hold back from getting to know others and entering into life together. We did not wait for community to reach out and serve us. Instead, we found ways to extend hospitality to others (something that I had been challenged to do at a retreat before we left Nicaragua). I believe this helped us avoid a victim mentality that is so easy to slip into. To judge the people around us for not being welcoming or caring enough about our past or transition.

We were open about our needs and asked for help. In a society that is individualistic this goes against the norm, but we reminded ourselves that if people do not know what we need they won't have the opportunity to help. We were pleasantly surprised by the willingness and genuine helpfulness of others.

When we needed to move our suitcases and furniture that we had accumulated over the summer from my sister-in-law's house to our on-campus apartment, three guys from the young adults group at our church (whom we had practically just met) volunteered their time and vehicles to move our family. There were several other people at the seminary ready and willing to carry our belongings up to our second story apartment. And a loaf of zucchini bread with a welcome note waiting on our kitchen counter.

In the coming weeks we would experience generosity and hospitality in the way of a laptop being given to Luke, textbooks being lent so they would not need to be purchased, and a double stroller being given to our family. We had come from an amazing community in Nicaragua, and it would have been easy to compare the two and project our assumptions on to our new one. But we were floored by the generosity and helpfulness of people we barely knew, and this rocked our stereotypes of people in the States.

Establishing routines was another big aide in our settling. Once school started and work schedules began, our family was able to enter into a "new normal." Daily and weekly routines greatly benefited our kids as well. Anything that was consistent was so good for them after having been in the chaos stage.

We did whatever we could do to maintain normalcy within our family, even on the practical level of bedtime routines. In Nicaragua, our kids were accustomed to going to bed with the sun which was about 6:30 pm. That made for a nice, quiet evening for tired parents, but of course it also meant that they were up with the sun (around 6:00 am). We decided to keep this routine as much as possible even during the summer time when the sun doesn't go down until almost 9:00 pm sometimes. It was difficult at first but they got used to it, and it was one more thing that did not change in their lives.

Getting on a new schedule and routine isn't always easy, and some can handle it easier than others. For my husband he can flip a switch in his brain so to speak. This is how we do things in Nicaragua. This is how we do things in the United States. Sometimes just practically recognizing that and not trying to assimilate and understand the two is so helpful.

I believe that giving ourselves time and space to adjust has been crucial. We have to recognize that it wasn't overnight that we got used to life overseas. It will take time here as well. Continuing to give our kids the space to talk about what they miss about Nicaragua has been so helpful to them as well. After we had been in Colorado for about four months, my three year old, Emily randomly said in the car, "I want to go back to Nicaragua." She had a sad face and repeated her statement, adding *"right now."* It's almost as if she was saying, "This was a fun little vacation and change of pace but I'm ready to go home now. When are we going back?" It has been healthy to continue engaging our kids in dialogue over the change they are experiencing rather than assuming all is well after a few months.

We've had to remind ourselves that friendships will take time as well. In a missionary community where you are practically thrown together and depend on each other for so much, friendship and intimacy run deep and fast. While we are open and willing to meet people and enter into their lives, the way friendships are established here is generally a much slower process and that's okay.

Also important to note is the way friendships and churches naturally change during the time overseas. If you are returning to the same place you lived in before moving overseas, be prepared that it is not the same. It has changed and you have changed. Preparing yourself for this is key and grieving what once was is normal. A missionary friend of mine puts it this way, "It is lonely because no one really knows you anymore nor it is fair to expect them to. However the longing remains - to be understood and known by those you were once so connected to before."

In this settling stage we are giving ourselves the freedom to enjoy the new and reassuring ourselves that doesn't mean we are betraying the old. We are hanging pictures on our walls. We are creating a home while not forgetting our previous one. Nicaragua continues to be in our hearts, a sweet memory that we look back on frequently. However, we have embraced this new life, filled with new adventures, new routines, and new people. And it is good. Our roots are growing again. We remember that ultimately we won't and shouldn't feel completely settled anywhere because our true home is in Heaven.

Chapter 12
What's Still Strange

After a year of being in the United States we are feeling more settled, yet aspects of life in this country still feel strange to us, and might for a long time. Having a dishwasher is one of them. We have used ours a grand total of three times. And the first time we attempted to run it, our good friend who had lived many years in Nicaragua but now lives in the States helped us remember how to work it. Using a dishwasher is honestly not a habit of ours, and something we got quite used to going without in Nicaragua.

Checking the mail each day is another one. We've gotten a little better at this, but in the beginning a few days would go by before we realized we hadn't checked the mail. *People do this every day?* we thought. In Nicaragua that was not a daily habit for us since there was no reliable mail system. The occasional package, birthday card or Christmas card was delivered to our school and would show up in our teacher box.

Checking the weather every day was another habit we were not used to at all. Only a few months into our time in Colorado, I wrote about this in a journal entry:

September 1, 2016

Something I noticed recently is why people pay attention to the weather here...they have to know how to dress or what to send their kids in as they head to school. Because [lightbulb moment] the temperature outside and in their houses is not the same. In Nicaragua we never paid attention to the weather. One, because it didn't change much and two, because if it did change slightly we would know it because it feels similar inside and outside our house. We never had to rely on weather apps or the weather channel to know how to dress.

One day we told our five year old son David that it was going to snow the next day, and his response was "What? Did God tell you that?" He had no concept of weathermen or weather channels. His mindset had always been: what you see is what you get, and it is whatever God chooses. He had no understanding of weather predictions.

Another thing we're still getting used to is the abundance of automatic systems and devices. Our kids have been fascinated by the many automatic devices they encounter in their world daily. Automatic doors, automatic toilets, automatic sinks, automatic hand dryers. You name it. They love it.

It's been strange to get used to there not being a pharmacy on practically every street corner. *Where do we go to buy cough drops or cold medicine?* We eventually figured out that we had to think of pharmacies or medical supplies as being part of grocery stores and gas stations. It was so strange to us that there were no stand-alone pharmacies we could just pop into. Even Walgreens or CVS had so much extra merchandise in them that it didn't feel like a pharmacy to us. These kind of stores felt almost equivalent to a supermarket in Nicaragua.

One day we thought back to our short route from school to home in Nicaragua and counted that there were seven pharmacies that we could potentially stop into. Each one is small and feels personal; you talk with the pharmacist and get what you need (usually with no prescription required). Perhaps the reason there are so many scattered around is because most people do not have vehicles. It may sound so unimportant, but we still do feel a bit disoriented and unglued not to see pharmacies at every corner.

The effect of weather and seasons on our community is another big adjustment we are still dealing with. It was strange that during the winter months we didn't see many people on campus. Of course this was also due to a busy time of finals and the Christmas season and families traveling. But nonetheless it's taken some getting used to. We're accustomed to seeing people all the time in tropical weather. We seemed to go months with seeing a few people occasionally, but other than that most people would stick indoors. It's been an adjustment for our kids to be indoors. We even bought a $5 mini trampoline at a garage sale to help them get their energy out in the winter, and that was a lifesaver!

Pumping our own gas at gas stations is also very different. Not having that interaction with an actual person is so strange. It's just me and my card and the pump. Also not having a *vulcanización* on every corner. Where do I go if I need a flat tire repaired or a quick check on air pressure?

One of the biggest aspects of life in this country that is still very unsettling and strange to us is the abundance of everything. And I'm not just talking about aisles of cereal choices or the incredible amount of retail stores or fast food restaurants. I'm talking about excess. And the availability of help for low-income families. It is amazing and overwhelming. There are countless opportunities for food assistance, medical aid, subsidies for heating bills, etc. I've been overwhelmed by the abundance at food banks. Many times we are loaded up with so much food, so much that will expire soon that will have to be thrown out anyway. Our family was even blessed by a nonprofit organization with free passes and classes at a local community recreation center. Help with paying for application fees for Colorado licenses, free clothes, toys, furniture, you name it.

And the Christmas gifts. That was a whole different story. I felt a little sick and unsettled in my stomach by all the options that were available to our family. Yes, I'm very grateful and it was an incredible help to our family, but it was overwhelming to have to say "no" to about six organizations or churches that were offering Christmas gifts for our kids. And the one church that we did accept gifts from showered us with many expensive gifts for each kid!

It brought up in our minds the whole concept and understanding of poverty. We know that we are a low-income family right now while Luke is studying full time and even with the side jobs I'm able to work, our expenses outweigh our income. But does that make us poor? Maybe by comparison our kids do not have all the gadgets and newest technologies and toys that other families can afford but really, does that make us worse off?

I thought of Nicaragua and other third world countries. Nicaragua knows poverty. A high percentage of the country is living off around a dollar a day of income. We're not poor. We don't *need* gifts like they need food and shelter and basic life provisions. And I couldn't help but wish that all this excess could be shared with them, not people who don't really need it.

As we continue moving through this settling stage, we're reminding ourselves to continue processing our grief while embracing new joys and experiences. We're giving ourselves pep talks that many times this transition can take years. And we're looking forward to the day when we can visit Nicaragua again.

I've heard from so many people that going back to your host country for a visit is a healing, healthy part of transition. One friend recently told me that her trip back to Nicaragua was surprisingly confirming to her that she had made the right decision and her time in Nicaragua was done. She said that she had tended to look back with questions and wondering if she should have stayed. I've heard from others that it is healthy to revisit the host country because you can see the changes right before your eyes. A place is never stagnant. People come and go. The country, the policies, the people, the structures change. It is good and healthy to see this with your own eyes.

I think the main thing during this settling stage is recognizing that it is a process, and we'll never really be "normal" Americans again. Living overseas has changed us, shaped us, forever altered our thinking. And it's okay that we won't fit back into the mold of what it means to be an American. That we will probably always have these struggles with how life is lived here or what the values and thought processes are.

But I want to be careful about letting pride lead me to judging others and elevating myself. I've known this pride throughout my life as a missionary kid. This feeling that I am better because I know or that I am wiser because I've been abroad. I want to be careful of that tendency and instead, be open to relationships with others, learn from them, and seek opportunities to share my insights and stories in a humble way.

And so we're settled. Our roots are growing down little by little. We are finding meaning and purpose and friends and answers to prayer. And yet there are still aspects of this new life that are very strange, that we're not used to. And that's okay. We live through them, choose to laugh, and figure out a way to cope. Because we've made it. And we've done it well.

Chapter 13
Letters to Family

I include these letters to my family here as a window into the memories and the connectedness our family had to Nicaragua and to each other. Here I grieve and process and celebrate and honor the moments I shared with the people I love in the land that I love.

Dear Luke,

It's hard to believe that almost twelve years ago we met for the first time in Nicaragua. In a place that seems so far away now. It's pretty strange to think back to those days. When we were young, awkwardly trying to figure out our dating drama, when the world seemed to revolve around us and our love story.

So many memories, both fun and hard. Some memories have faded, but many are still so present in my mind. It's like they happened yesterday. Like the time we decided to take the new-to-you car out for a "test drive" at midnight only to be stranded in the middle of an intersection when it quit running. Those policemen must have thought we were crazy gringos. I still laugh when I think about how they made you do a breath test and how we didn't have any cash on us so we "paid" them in phone cards to tow the car to school. And I laugh even harder when I think about how the next day we found out that the simple problem was that we had run out of gas (except that the gas gauge didn't work properly so we hadn't known it).

I love remembering good times of traveling together and adventures with friends. Burning holes in tennis shoes from stepping on hot lava at Volcan Pacaya. Long bus rides to Guatemala or Costa Rica. "Skiing" down the side of Cerro Negro and emptying rocks out of our shoes at the bottom. Eating tortillas and refried beans out of a bag so that we could afford the next nights' stay on the road. I remember when we lived in our first house the yard was so small that you actually cut the grass with a weedeater instead of a lawn mower. And you would get so mad at me if I accidentally threw a frisbee or a ball over the wall while I was playing fetch with Bella.

Later our experiences shifted to more family memories as we began to have kids. Taking them to the beach, going on walks in our neighborhood, running in 5K races with strollers and a leash for Bella. All of these memories and more color my history with you. What a fun, exciting, blessed, and rich history in Nicaragua we can look back on together. I know there were not-so-fun memories as well. Like when you got dengue fever and the itching was unbearable. Or when you got stung by a scorpion while changing David's diaper. Or the conflicts with coworkers and misunderstandings with students' parents. Or the deaths of loved ones both near and far or the changes in relationships. But we went through these experiences together.

Over our years of living life in Nicaragua I've seen you grow so much, Luke. You were an outspoken, passionate, adventurous, and social single guy when we met all those years ago. I've seen you develop into a mature, patient and wise man who is an excellent leader, discipler, husband and father. I've loved being in the front row seat and being able to watch how your experiences and your God have shaped you into who you are today. How the trials in Nicaragua, conflict with parents and team members have taught you much compassion and patience. I've appreciated how you've grown in the area of self-control, and I can see how God has really helped you harness the passion He's given you and you've been able to use it for good. And I've been impressed with how you've grown in the area of making tough decisions, seeking God's will for your life and walking in confidence.

I'm so very proud of the way you have led our family in this new season of our lives. Your intentionality with leaving Nicaragua well has helped us all have a much smoother transition than it might have been otherwise. I'm full of pride at the way you have embraced a new role and new life. How you have entered into your studies with excitement and joy and how you have welcomed new people in your life. I love seeing your openness to whatever God has for our family. And I'm especially grateful for your encouragement and support of me writing this book.

I miss making memories with you in our home of Nicaragua. I miss being in a familiar place we both love. But I'm glad we can make memories in a new home and that we can preserve our old ones. My prayer for you is that you will always find ways to stay connected to Nicaragua. I know it is a very special place for you, one that has been part of your life since you were eleven years old. That you would be able to look back on our time in Nicaragua with joy and no regrets. And I pray that as you bury old dreams that God would birth new passions and visions in you. I'm so glad you chose to commit to that second year of teaching at our school so I could meet you. Nicaragua and I will never be the same after knowing you.

Love,
Ellen

Dear David Luke,

Have I ever told you the story of how Daddy and I met? Well, you know how you were born in Nicaragua? Well, Daddy and I met in Nicaragua six years before you were born, can you believe that? Do you remember the Quinta Allyson apartments? That's where some of your friends lived. When Mommy first came to Nicaragua, that's where I lived. So, I had only been in Nicaragua for a few days, and I had met new friends. You know who they were? Aunt Maggie and Uncle Jason! They had come to teach at the same school as I did. Aunt Maggie taught second grade, and Uncle Jason taught math and science to middle school kids. So, it was about 6:30 at night, and I was swimming in the pool at Quinta Allyson with my new friends, Aunt Maggie and Uncle Jason when all of the sudden I heard somebody on the side of the pool say to us, "Hey! You guys shouldn't be swimming in here after 6:00 pm; it's against the apartment rules." That was Daddy saying that! But I had never met him before. I figured out he was probably Aunt Maggie's older brother because of the way he was bossing her around (kinda like how you make sure your younger sisters are following the rules, right?) My first thought about Daddy was, "Wow, I guess this is Aunt Maggie's brother. He sure is bossy." And that's how we met.

After that we became friends and hung out a lot together and with our other friends. We had a lot of fun adventures together, and we traveled a lot. One time we took a bus to Guatemala and we stayed with Grammie and GrandDad. The more time Mommy and Daddy spent together the more we realized we loved each other. We shared many things in common, like music, sports, our faith in Jesus, and traveling.

After we dated we decided to get married. We were still living in Nicaragua, but our wedding was in Indiana at Grandma's church. We had a reception in Nicaragua, though, where all our friends could celebrate with us. The first house we lived in was nearby Quinta Allyson. A little more than a year after we got married, we got Bella. She was almost one year old and a beautiful dog. Bella was like our first kid. We loved her. We had so much fun with her, playing in the yard, taking her on walks, chasing her around trying to give her a bath, putting her toy rope in the tree and seeing how high she could jump to get it. But you know what? Having a dog was fun, but we really wanted to have a baby. And so we prayed that God would give us a baby.

A few months after we moved into a different house, we found out that we were pregnant with YOU! You grew and grew in my tummy. We decided not to find out if you were a girl or a boy. We wanted to be surprised when you came out. You know what almost every Nicaraguan told me though? They would touch my belly and look at its shape, and they would say "Es niño." I don't know how they could tell, but they all guessed you were a boy. And so you were born in Managua, Nicaragua on July 13, 2011. Daddy and I were so excited to meet you and find out if you were a girl or a boy. As soon as you were born we heard the doctor exclaim "varoncito!"

We did many things with you as a baby. You went to the beach for the first time when you were only six days old. We took you everywhere. And it's a good thing that everyone loves babies in Nicaragua. People were constantly touching you, commenting on your white skin, calling you "chelito" and holding you. Every Nicaraguan I knew gave me advice on what I should or shouldn't eat because you had colic. That means you would cry and scream (even if you had a clean diaper and were fed) a lot of the day.

I loved watching you grow, and I loved seeing you enjoy our little house. You learned to crawl and walk on our cold tile floor. Many days you would only wear a diaper because it was so hot. We played outside a lot and had picnics in our backyard. We have a lot of videos of you when you were little, and there are birds singing in the background. We had a beautiful place to live, and you were comfortable there. I remember the times that I would do "kid exchanges" with our neighbors who had two boys your age. You would go over to play at their house for a little bit, or their boys would come over to our house. Sometimes we would pass you guys right over the fence!

You loved Bella and she loved you. She learned to be gentle with you and let you pet her and crawl all over her. She was very protective of you, even before you were born. As you grew we loved seeing you pick up on Spanish words. We saw you at a young age start to make sense of this interesting life you were born into. You began to understand that you had a big family full of cousins and playmates in Indiana and relatives in Texas and Colorado and your grandparents in Guatemala and your own family in Nicaragua. You were flexible and were thrilled to travel on airplanes. Then you began to make friends of your own and not just sit beside them in nursery playing with toys. Entering Mincaito, your all-Spanish preschool, was a big deal, and we were so proud of you for getting better at Spanish.

I know leaving Nicaragua was hard, and it wasn't so fun to say goodbye to your good friends. And it was also very sad to leave Bella. Mommy is sad that you can't do anymore motorcycle rides with Daddy or that we can't stop to eat pupusas on the way home from preschool. I'm disappointed you won't be around constant Spanish and that as you say, "I'm forgetting my Spanish." No more playing at the beach with Bella or playing on a dusty playground set while Daddy plays ultimate frisbee on Saturday mornings.

I will miss those fun memories for you. But I want you to know that I am so proud of you for having a good attitude and a thankful heart as you said goodbye to the friends and people you loved. I am so proud of you for giving away some of your favorite toys to your friends. I know that was so hard for you, and you did an awesome job! You were a wonderful big brother, helping your sisters understand what was going on. And I'm so proud of you for praying for new friends in Colorado and then noticing and thanking God when He answered those prayers!

My prayer for you, David, is that you will never forget your first five years of life in Nicaragua. That your heart will always have a place for the country of your birth and the people in it. I hope that you can visit again some day and see where you lived, where you went to school, where we were a family together. I pray that you will be curious about your past and ask Daddy and I any questions you have about Nicaragua. And I pray that you would recognize that all of God's people all around the world are special to Him. I pray that you would not get too comfortable in the United States, this place of abundance where there is so much to see, enjoy, buy. May you not walk after the things of this world but after God's heart for you and others. I love you, David, and I'm so glad you were able to start your life in the beautiful country of Nicaragua among its friendly and warm people. God has been so good to our family, and I pray that through the years you will see that.

Love you,
Mama

Dear Emily Kay,

I'm so glad you were born into our family. When you came along, you already had a big brother and a dog and a Mommy and Daddy who had been living in Managua, Nicaragua for nine years. Ask David to read you my letter to him about how Mommy and Daddy met, okay?

When David was a baby in Mommy's tummy, we decided not to find out if he was going to be a boy or a girl. But when we found out we were pregnant with you, Mommy convinced

Daddy that we should find out if you were a boy or a girl. And you were a girl!

When Nicaraguans found out we were going to have a girl, they were satisfied that we would have our little "parejita" (our little pair of boy and girl). They told me again (like they had told me when I was pregnant with David) that they could tell by the shape of my belly that I was having a girl.

You were actually born two weeks early! We brought you to our little home that was almost finished being expanded. I guess all the noise, the banging, the construction noises didn't bother you one bit because you slept right through it. You loved to sleep so much! Your brother adored you, and Bella was happy to have another little kid to lick and be protective of. You got attention everywhere we went. You fit right into our family and our home.

When David started going to Mincaito, you wanted to go too, even though you were only two and a half. We waited until about a month before you turned three to put you in at Mincaito and were you ever ready! You walked in there as confidently as ever with your little purse around your shoulder, and you didn't even look back. No tears at all. You were ready for this. You loved preschool, and you did really well there. It was incredible how much you adapted and how much Spanish you learned. We were so proud of you!

Our family had so many adventures in Nicaragua together. I loved seeing your smiling face as you chased waves at the beach and as we rocked back and forth in a boat touring the islands of Granada. One year for Daddy's birthday we decided to go to San Juan del Sur for the weekend to run in a

6K race. We took the double jogging stroller with you and David in it! Part of the race was on the beach. It was so fun to make that memory all together. You liked going to the grocery store with me and talking to the checkout lady. You always wanted to tag along to school for lunch with Daddy.

Do you remember one time we were going on a family walk in our neighborhood, and we passed by a house that had little puppies they were giving away. We stopped so you and David and Lucy could pet the puppies. But the longer we stayed we had this crazy idea come into our heads. What if we brought a puppy home? There was one more left, a cute little black one with white tips on his tail and paws. And the owner said it had to be gone that day! Mommy and Daddy made the quick decision to take the puppy home, but our plan was to watch him for the weekend but then give him away on Monday to a friend of ours who had wanted a dog. And so we did! And you loved this little puppy to death! You carried him around and made sure he had food and drink. We called it our "weekend puppy" since we were only taking care of it for the weekend. You were sad to say goodbye when the time came. It was a fun little preview of what it would be like to have a puppy, and Daddy and I laugh because we went out on a walk that day not planning at all to come home with a little pet!

I'm sad that you'll miss out on learning more Spanish. And it makes me even more sad to see you losing the Spanish you had. I loved that you spoke to me a lot in Spanish when we first moved back to the States. I had no idea you knew so much! It grieves me to think you won't be growing up with your friends. It makes me want to cry to think that you won't live in our beautiful house where you loved to run outside in the grass and climb trees and give Bella baths.

But I am so proud of you, Emily. I'm proud of you for being able to move at such a young age and say goodbye to your home. You have lived in four houses in your young four year old life! I'm proud of you for learning Spanish and doing so well at Mincaito. For loving Nicaragua and your teachers and friends. I'm so thankful that you are still talking about Nicaragua and your life there.

My prayer for you is that you would somehow keep up your Spanish. I don't know how, but I really hope we can figure out how to do this for you and with you. I don't want you to lose it completely. I hope and pray that you will remember where you came from and how your life started in a country far away. I pray you wouldn't forget the faces and the places. And I pray that you would keep loving others who are different from you and that you would have a bigger picture of the world than just our new home in Littleton, Colorado.

Love,
Mom

Dear Lucy Katherine,

Your history with Nicaragua is interesting. Technically your life began there, but you didn't live there until you were eight months old. Mommy found out she was pregnant with you a few months before we moved to Indiana for a year of furlough. We were not planning on having a baby while we were in the States for that short time, but God had different plans. And we're so glad He did!

You were born in Carmel, Indiana into a different situation than your brother and sister. We were temporarily living in a house that was owned by kind friends of ours. You were welcomed into the world by many cousins, aunts and uncles, and grandparents. Your siblings didn't have that privilege when they were born in Nicaragua. As you grew you experienced a lot of relatives around, the cold Indiana weather, and a family that was in transition. Around the time you were six or seven months, we began to start planning to go back to Nicaragua where Mommy and Daddy had lived for eleven years.

When we got back to Nicaragua you were eight months old, and everyone there was so excited to meet you! They had seen your pictures, but they were so eager to see you in person. And they already loved you before they had even met you. We were so glad that you traveled well and adapted well to life in Nicaragua. You did a little more crying than normal at first, but you soon got used to your new environment and you were off to the races with crawling around on our tile floors and exploring all around the house!

I loved seeing how much you enjoyed our home. It was the perfect setup for you. You could roam in and out doors, giggling as you entered each room. You loved to tag along after your older siblings and Bella. You were so cute whenever your ears would perk up at the sound of a chirping gecko. You loved to run and greet your Daddy at the gate when you heard his motorcycle horn.

Even though you only spent a little over a year in Nicaragua, we had so much fun seeing you grow and make many memories there. You learned to walk in Nicaragua. You preferred going without shoes whenever you could. I remember specifically that you took the most steps in the row at the "newish" playgrounds down by the port. We were so proud of you! Being dedicated at our international church on your one-year birthday was also a special moment for us. Even though we had the opportunity to dedicate you in Indiana at a younger age, we chose to do it in Nicaragua, where our community had been and was. Your older brother and sister had been dedicated at the same church.

I remember where you said your first word. We were at Laguna de Apoyo, and you saw a dog and said, "Bella!" Oh how you loved Bella. You would constantly be climbing over her, chasing her around, and never ceasing to say "Bella, Bella, Bella." And she was so gentle with you. Allowing you to tug at her ears and tail, spray her with water, lean into her. She loved the attention you gave her.

Another fun memory I have of you is when our family was at a conference with our mission at Selva Negra (a retreat center in the mountains a few hours north of Managua). The conference had just ended and most families were headed back to the city, but we decided to stick around for a few hours longer to enjoy the cooler weather and go on a family horseback ride. Our guide had David with him on his horse, I took Emily on mine with me, and Daddy had you on his horse with him. All of you three kids loved the horse rides, but you especially were delighted! You started giggling and giggling from the very beginning. But after a while you had gotten pretty quiet. You started feeling pretty heavy to Daddy and sure enough, you had fallen fast asleep!

One not-so-fun memory was when a scorpion stung you one day. I heard you in your crib crying during nap time. I waited a few minutes to see if you would settle back down, but your crying got louder. So I went in to check on you. I got you out of the crib and held you, but you would not stop crying. I checked on the toys in the crib to see if you had gotten hurt somehow. I couldn't figure out anything. I brought you out to the toy room, and then all of the sudden I heard a plop on the floor. I looked down and it was a big black, evil-looking scorpion. You were still crying and then I began to panic. I ran into the kitchen with you in my arms to grab the phone to call Daddy. He ordered me to get back into the toy room and kill that scorpion! When we ran back in there, the scorpion was nowhere to be found. It took you a while to calm down, and I did not put you back in your crib that day. Neither did I venture back into the toy room or your room until Daddy got home. He couldn't find the scorpion anywhere. Thankfully you were okay other than the scare of it all. For a few weeks after that traumatic experience, you would wake up in the night and cry for Mommy (which was not normal for you). We began praying over you every night when we put you to bed, and that helped a lot and eventually you stopped crying in the night.

I'm so proud of you for being flexible and going with the flow. For learning to love a new environment at such a young age. It was obvious that you felt safe and loved by your family, and so you enjoyed doing everything that we did. I'm proud of you for embracing another new environment now that we've moved back to the States. For staying close to your family and still bringing us daily joy by that goofiness that is so much a part of who you are.

I am sad that you will miss out on growing up in Nicaragua. So many things I wish you could experience. Going to Mincaito. Learning Spanish. Experiencing the TCK (Third Culture Kid) life with all of its benefits and challenges. Appreciating true beauty and hopefully grasping the meaning of raw joy. I'm sad that the rich history that our family has been part of will not be in your daily life. It makes me grieve to think that you won't know where your family has spent most of our lives up until this point. And I'm sad that you won't know the people who dearly loved you and cared for you at such a young age. Our "empleada" adored you and you delighted in her. She was such a gentle and patient caretaker. You brought her so much joy and laughter during her time in our home. You also learned quickly to be her helper and followed her all over the house. I know it broke her heart when she had to say goodbye to you. Because she knew that you would grow and you would forget. The hours, the days she poured into you. How she held you, fed you, changed you, loved on you, spoke to you. I want you to know that there could have never been anyone else more suited to help Mommy in taking care of you. I always trusted her, and you were always so excited when she would ring our doorbell. I am so grateful to our "empleada," and I'm so glad you had the blessing of being with her, a kind, godly woman who loved you very much.

My prayer for you is that you would somehow know your history and appreciate it. That you would be interested in Nicaragua and our past. That you would ask questions and be curious. And that you would be thankful for the short window of time that you spent in Nicaragua. I hope that you won't forget everything about your brief home but that we can keep something alive in your heart and mind. And I pray that you would not be satisfied with the status quo but always be looking for adventures and ways that God will you lead you outside of what everyone expects.

I wish I could preserve all those memories for you, Lucy. But hopefully I have preserved a few. Know that we love Nicaragua and we love you. And we loved that you could be part of it for a short time. Don't forget that even that brief time in your young life was a gift from God and according to His purposes.

Love,
Mommy

Dear Elizabeth Kate,

You have no idea what kind of family you have been born into. Our history is interesting and unconventional to say the least. I hope that you will learn how your Mommy and Daddy met and that you will know the details about how we even ended up in Nicaragua in the first place. I hope that you will learn about the place that your family spent most of our time until now.

I wish you could see first-hand this place that will always be in our hearts, Nicaragua. And experience the people and the weather and the sights and the sounds. All the things that became so familiar to us. It was our life. But it's so strange to think that you did not experience it with us.

So while I am sad that you will not know and see and experience and live our family's history in Nicaragua, I am excited for the story that God has for you. His timing is perfect and He knows the days that are laid out for you. I hope and pray that you will learn about your family's history and develop an interest in Nicaragua. But I also hope and pray that you develop your own hopes and dreams. That you follow who God will form you to be.

You are loved and there are many people here and in Nicaragua who love you already.

Love,
Mommy

Action Points for
Part Three: The Settling

Chapter 11:

For missionaries*:

1. Determine to keep a sense of adventure and sense of humor.
2. Have fun exploring your new home; get a library card; look for a new park.
3. List ways you can extend hospitality to others and then act on them.
4. Do your part in finding a community to be part of.
5. Establish consistent but flexible family routines.

For family, friends, and supporters:

1. Encourage but do not push your missionary to be involved in your community and to establish routines.
2. Offer consistent hospitality but recognize when space is needed.
3. Keep praying for your missionary as they continue settling.

* I use the term "missionaries" because that was my context and my experience. However, these action points apply to a broader range of people: expats, embassy workers, military, and global workers of any kind.

Resource List

Debriefing:

Debriefing and Renewal Program at Mission Training International - mti.org/dar
Mission Training International, located in beautiful Palmer Lake, Colorado, offers an one week debriefing and renewal program to missionaries who have been overseas. It is for either missionaries on a furlough, who plan to return to the field, or for those who are transitioning from the field to their home country. We highly recommend this resource as we attended in July of 2014.

Godspeed Resources Connection - godspeedservices.org
Godspeed Resources Connection helps missionaries find housing for up to one year and provide counseling or debriefing for individuals, couples, families, and teams. They also provide Shepherds Rest for physical and spiritual rest, referrals and requests for professional services, and on-field care. The website also offers partnership opportunities, information about their Columbia, South Carolina location, and about their ministry.

Narramore Christian Foundation - ncfliving.org
Narramore Christian Foundation is a global ministry whose mission is to meet the psychological needs of underserved populations based on the integration of psychology and Scripture. Their website offers

information about their seminars and trainings including a two week MK Reentry seminar, counseling centers, psychology for living resources, news, events, and how to support.

Organized Retreats:

Thrive Ministry - thriveministry.org
Thrive is an organization that hosts retreats for North American women serving overseas at a very low cost. They usually offer a retreat in Colorado each summer and each year they host a few other retreats in different regions of the world. I highly recommend their retreats; I attended the Colorado retreat in 2016.

Abide Reentry Retreat at Train International - traininternational.org/TRAIN_International/Abide.html
Train International says that they are equipping for cross-cultural effectiveness. They have a one-week renewal for those transitioning back into American culture and debriefs the cross-cultural experience, explores reverse culture shock, and equips for healthy re-entry into the home culture. The website gives information about the retreat and how to register for it. It is located in Joplin, Missouri.

Interaction International - interactionintl.org/transition.asp
Interaction International claims that they are today's voice for third culture kids and internationally mobile families. They offer camps for missionary kids including a re-entry refresher, caregiver trainings, and transition seminars. My siblings and I attended a re-entry camp organized by Interaction International; this was an integral part of our adjustment back to the United States.

Guest Houses and Retreat Centers:

Missionary Care Ministry - missionarycareministry.org
This organization owns and runs a beautiful guesthouse on a 11

acres partly-wooded property in. It is a peaceful environment located near Athens, Georgia. They offer the guesthouse free of charge to missionaries that are on furlough or returning from their overseas field. The website has information about their guesthouse, pictures, FAQs, availability, reservations and how to volunteer or donate. We have stayed there and really enjoyed the experience.

Shelter Pines - shelterpines.org
Shelter Pines provides a place where weary warriors can recover their energy and renew their vision; a place where they can reconnect as families, and linger with Jesus, so that He can meet with them and speak to their soul and spirit. It's a safe place to rest, walk, pray, read, play with your kids, get re-acquainted with your spouse, evaluate, renew and regroup. Missionary friends of ours are helping with Shelter Pines and believe in it's importance for offering missionaries rest and renewal.

Alongside Inc. - alongsidecares.net
A counseling-focused retreat ministry for pastors and missionaries who desire restoration and renewal. They host the retreats at a beautiful facility near Kalamazoo, Michigan. The resources offered on their website includes a ministry toolbox which is a collection of articles, a collection of newsletters, prayer support, recommended reading, and a list of websites related to their ministry.

Heartstream Resources - heartstreamresources.org
Heartstream Resources provides education/prevention programs as well as programs of restoration and renewal for cross-cultural workers. Their website includes a missionary retreat center, professional papers, FAQs, program information, radio programs, books and DVD resources.

Counseling:

Linkcare - linkcare.org
Linkcare has Christian Counselors who provide care for missionaries, pastors, Christian workers and their families, and the people in Fresno, California. It offers residential treatment there as well as on-field services abroad. Their website has resources, media, and offer a retreat housing option. My family knows the counselors personally and highly recommend this resource.

Directory of International Therapists - internationaltherapistdirectory.com
This website offers a directory of more than 200 English speaking professional mental health therapists who are familiar with the international expatriate experiences in 50 countries around the world. Not only can you find a therapist, but there is information of how to become a member, FAQs, a forum, and a blog.

Marble Retreat - marbleretreat.org
A retreat center offering 8-day intensive counseling programs for pastors and missionaries. Located in the picturesque Crystal River Valley of the Colorado Rockies has been set aside for rest, healing, and life transformation. Their website offers articles and ministry resources, news, a blog, program information, and how to donate.

Other Organizations:

Barnabas International - barnabas.org
Barnabas International is an organization that provides people that are passionate about caring for global workers through going, speaking, listening, and giving. Their website offers free resource books, care for global workers, resources and trainings, upcoming events, information about their retreats and conferences including

their debriefing retreat for global workers, called Interlude and ELIM, a six day retreat for global workers and their families for rest, reflection, recovery and renewal.

Families in Global Transitions - www.figt.org
Families in Global Transition is a welcoming forum for globally mobile individuals, families, and those working with them. Their website offers a blog, information about their annual conference, monthly webinars, newsletters, list of free resources, upcoming events, and how to support.

Servant Care - servantcare.com/hospitality/hhList.php
Servant Care lists homes state by state that offer hospitality for missionaries for short term stay. This website offers resources for cars, books, and computers.

Books:

- *Who Moved My Cheese?* By: Spencer Johnson
- *Re-entry* By: Peter Jordan
- *Looming Transitions* By: Amy Young
- *Returning Well* By: Melissa Chaplin

Other websites that contain a list of valuable resources:

- missionarycare.com/links.html
- linkcare.org/resources
- alongsidecares.net/resources/links
- rockyreentry.com/debriefing-expat-reentry-resources-missionaries
- marbleretreat.org/additional-resources-marble-retreat/#__ministry

About the Author

Ellen Rosenberger has lived most of her life in the Latin American countries of Bolivia and Nicaragua. She grew up as a missionary kid in Santa Cruz, Bolivia from the age of four until she graduated in 2000 from Santa Cruz Christian Learning Center. In 2004, she received a Bachelor of Arts in TESOL (Teaching English to Speakers of Other Languages) from Moody Bible Institute in Chicago, Illinois. Ellen moved to Managua, Nicaragua in 2005 where she met her husband, Luke. She taught English Language Learning and Pre-School at Nicaragua Christian Academy until 2011, when she became a mom.

Luke and Ellen have four kids: David (6), Emily (4½), Lucy (3), and Elizabeth (9 months). Their youngest was born during the writing and editing of this book. When she's not feeding, clothing, or reading to one of her children, Ellen enjoys writing, reading, hiking, and watching "The Voice." Ellen published her first book in May of 2016, called *Missionaries Are Real People*. Soon after, the Rosenberger family moved from Nicaragua to Colorado, where Luke is pursuing a Master of Divinity degree at Denver Seminary.

Thank You

Thank you for purchasing my book! I would love for you to recommend it to other missionaries, friends and families of missionaries, churches, and mission organizations. It is my hope that this book would be a valuable resource to many.

Would you consider leaving an honest review on Amazon sharing what inspired, encouraged, or challenged you? Reviews are super important to the success of self-published books. Thank you so much!

You may be wondering how in the world I, as a mom of four, was able to write and publish a book. In addition to the incredible support of my husband and many friends, this is how: I took a course called "Self Publishing for First Time Authors" from Self-Publishing School. I would hands-down recommend this program. They gave me the tools that I needed to embark on this journey and see it to completion! I'm so grateful to Chandler Bolt and his team for running an excellent program that focuses on empowering aspiring authors.

If you love to write and have ever thought of writing a book some day, let me tell you: you can! If I can, you can! Check out Self-Publishing School and if you decide that it's for you, please use this link to let them know that I referred you: https://xe172.isrefer.com/go/curcust/ellenrosenberger

More from Ellen Rosenberger

Reviews for *Missionaries Are Real People*:

"This is a real book by a real missionary who is brave enough to share her experiences. It's a must read for anyone who is contemplating becoming a missionary or is already serving."

"Excellent portrayal of the life of missionaries."

"Honest, practical and easy to read. Churches, supporters, friends, family and missionaries themselves need to read this."

"This wonderful book is very easy to read, and draws you in like having a conversation with a close friend. Her practical examples and real life experiences make the author so relatable; she will have you laughing and crying, sometimes at the same time."

Paperback and Kindle editions are available on Amazon.

Made in the USA
Columbia, SC
11 November 2019